LIFE
LOVES
ME,
LIFE
LOVES
ME
NOT

MIRELA AJDIMOVSKI

ISBN: 9781725046467

Dedication

To all my friends and family from all over the world: the ones I encountered and lost; lost and found again; those who along the way in my thirty-two years, have come and departed; the relationships that have been torn apart and ones that grew stronger. Many of you have made me the worst and the best version of myself. I love you for being a part of my life.

I choose to live my life to the fullest—even with regrets—and, as a result, to learn some of life's most amazing lessons, ones that will teach me about who I want to become.

Believe in yourself, in your own power, and in your dreams; be passionate; do honorable and hard work. Be proud, be kind, share with others, love yourself, love others, and show gratitude for all the known and the unknown blessings. We are privileged to live a life with the people we love, and everything amazing surrounding us.

XOXO M.

Acknowledgements

To my dear parents: life has thrown at us so many *"Why me?"* moments. Struggle has played a major role. Despite all the circumstances and everything we have been through, I couldn't be prouder to call you Mom and Dad and to be your daughter. Each one of us has grown through the worst possible situations. At the end, we have been there for each other through all of it, even if it was from a distance. Thank you for everything you have always done for me, and I'm sorry for the times that I took you for granted.

To my brother, Amir: I miss you dearly, I wish things were different. Thank you for showing me what it means to have a sibling. Thank you for showing me the capability of strength and ability to love that one person can have. I pray every day you get better so one day you can hold your daughter in your arms again.

To my editor and my friend, Jacquie: thank you for your infinite help with making this book become a reality; I couldn't have done it without you. You have been a true inspiration and motivation in the past few years. Your kindness is above anything else.

Alla Famiglia Cavalli: thank you endlessly for giving Amir and me such a wonderful part of our childhood. Thank you for showing us the beauty of the world outside all the sadness. My world and my life are so much better because I have met you. Even with distance between us, I will truly never forget your kindness and love. Italy and the Cavalli residence will always hold a special place in my heart. I look forward to one day meeting with you again.

To my childhood friends: Amela, Ilda, Izeta and Alma—what an impact you have made on my life, and in the best way possible! I miss you every day; I thank you for being the best part of my childhood. You are always in my heart.

"In the beginning life loved me,
and I loved it back.
Then my wounds grew sore,
and life loved me no more.

I fought through the pain
with the help of a flower;
as I put it to my wounds,
it gave me strength and it gave me power.

Life will love you,
and life will love you not;
count every moment as a blessing,
even every battle that you fought.

MIRELA AJDIMOVSKI

Prologue

For as long as I can remember, I have been trying to make sense of—and understand—how exactly I ended up here in this bubble of chaos I call my life: how a girl like me is living in a world of possibilities with all the possible loose screws. I been angry, happy, anxious, afraid, and confident, sometimes all at once; and still attempting to figure out how to aim my-wildly-misunderstood-self in a proper direction. I have been forcing myself to accept the fact that my life, up until now, hasn't gone according to plan. It *has,* though, given me faith and a fighting chance to make it precisely how I want it to be.

We are all human beings, and none of us are immune to lousy days, bad experiences, or certain points in our lives that tend to drive us crazy. Life can be unbelievably cruel sometimes. We become vulnerable and let our guard down when things get hard. We let it drown us into exhaustion—and, most of the time, we let it push us into giving up.

This is our perfect opportunity to take action; to stand up to the weak parts of ourselves. Look in the mirror at the person staring back at you, wipe away those tears, and turn that frown upside down. Tell yourself, "I've got this." Don't fall to the level of a victim; be a warrior and believe. The world needs you.

The truth is, this kind of power of belief is not easy to come by. There are two paths to choose from: we either face the problem or we let it knock us down. It is simply up to us to determine which path we want to take. My daily routine starts with positive affirmations; it's a crucial and necessary element to include in your life. *Lead with confidence* they say. I hold the power to change the way I feel about any given situation. Bad things happen all the time. Even so, just because life works that way does not mean I need to let it control me. *I* get to control how I react emotionally about anything that happens. I choose to not awaken the negative feelings of self-pity within me, every single time something goes wrong. If you can't change the outcome, then shift the reaction and adjust your thoughts to live a more positive life. Never give up. Life should never be about avoiding problems either; I am in the process of learning this lesson the hard way. I know we all tend to do it—but, if we don't face our problems right away, they are just going to manifest into bigger issues or more bad feelings, and no one wants that. I surely don't.

We have become the world's best procrastinators and our own worst critics; however, it is also highly important to recognize our own strength. If we weren't strong enough to overcome life's hardest punches— from wars all over the world, crimes, poverty, cheating, losses, and major accidents to things as little as being late to work, hitting every damn red light, spilling coffee on your brand new outfit, or any of life's misfortunes that can make a day go from great to horrible—I don't think we would exist.

We were created out of armor, and I am not talking about the kind you wear to a battle to protect yourself. I am talking about the strength of our flesh and bones. The kind of armor that's been bruised repeatedly—yet possesses this amazing power of healing itself back to perfection.

Bad experiences and bad points in life are all a learning tool for the future, training our hearts to make us stronger and to be psychologically capable of accepting everything life throws at us. We can learn from each other no matter what happens in life, and most of all, we can overcome everything with patience, time, hard work, and willpower. Maintaining solid faith in our own capabilities is the necessary key to holding off on judging ourselves too harshly.

My life experience has come in hefty portions of both good and corrupt. I can't complain I am healthy, I am blessed with a roof over my head, I have a meal to eat every day, a job that (hardly) pays the bills, and amazing friends. I am also a daughter and a sister in a very dysfunctional family. I have a hard-earned degree that I don't use. Sometimes I am lonely, even when I am not alone—and the worst part is, *I still don't know what I am doing with my life.* I am on this difficult journey of figuring it all out. I am stuck between the past, present, and future and my avid attempt to put everything in its perfect place, creating an impossible goal for myself. Changing the past is out of the question, although I trust that the rest of my life will be the best of my life. Figuring out what you genuinely want out of life takes time, and *that's okay*.

I began to recognize how much I didn't appreciate what I already had. Writing my feelings down on paper certainly has put things in perspective for me. Most of my life, I had been over-analyzing all the bad luck— until I finally saw how extremely fortunate, I was. The good outweighs the bad. It always does. This forced me to become mindful of how much I had grown as a person, the painful things I had overcome, and the beautiful things I had experienced so far.

I sincerely believe knowledge is partly experience, but the other half comes from the people we experience it with, and only this life gives us the chance to learn and understand all our heart's desires.

The easiest thing in the world is to be negative about everything life throws at you, as negativity does not require any hard work. The hardest thing in the world is to be positive. All the great things in life, like honesty, trust, success, and relationships, require all the effort in the world.

We need to accept the challenge of life and apply positive traits to ourselves first before applying them to others. We need to learn to love ourselves, no matter how imperfect we are. Learn to enjoy your own company before being in the company of others, be happy with what you have, and for every negative thing, find five positives to ensure the positive always outweighs the negative. Exhale the negative and inhale the positive.

CHAPTER ONE

About a Girl

It was 1986, the Year of the Tiger. President Reagan led the United States of America, people listened to "The Greatest Love of All" by Whitney Huston, and *Rambo* was the most watched movie on TV. Four thousand five hundred and ninety-some miles away, I made my way into the world early Wednesday morning on the fourteenth of May. We lived in a little village called Orašje outside the city of Doboj in Bosnia and Herzegovina. My parents married at young ages in July of 1985. Mama, only nineteen, and Tata, just twenty-six, joined their life together as one.

Our house stood on top of the hill of our village. In Bosnia, villages are called *Selo*, and, when I think of our *Selo* back home, I think of muddy roads, animals everywhere, and clusters of houses grouped together. The next village is a hill or a valley over. As a kid, I would look down from the hill and see the entire stretch of village houses, their thick-bricked walls, and bright red-tiled rooves, faintly catching a glimpse of the city buildings through the fog.

Our first home was a small one-bedroom house. We didn't have a lot, but we had enough at that time. A long and narrow kitchen stood at front of the entrance with a wood-burning stove and a fridge in one corner. The eating nook was in front of the window with a view of the backyard. The spacious living room with little natural light had wooden paneling on the ceiling, multicolored wallpaper, a pull-out couch, and a one-color television. My younger brother and I shared the small bedroom.

Amir arrived into the world on December 4th, 1988. I can still remember the chilly winter morning I met my brother for the first time. Back in those days, they didn't allow family and friends to enter the maternity wing of the hospital due to health and safety reasons, so my dad snuck me around the hospital building and to the window of my mother's room.

Mom brought him to the window so I could finally meet my baby brother.

Amir has always been a strong kid: a persistent, loving heartbreaker with a heart of gold, nevertheless he was always full of energy! No matter how many times he fell of his tricycle bleeding, he would just stand up and do it all over again. One morning, we woke up to him crying after he climbed out of his crib and walked to the fridge to get his bottle. Mama found him on the floor in a puddle of milk, his little hands and feet glued to the piece of cardboard that my dad put under the fridge to trap the mice. He managed to knock everything out of the fridge; milk, eggs, and food had gone *everywhere*. Mama spent a few solid hours trying to clean the unpleasant combination of glue and food out of his hair and clothes.

Playing in the backyard is my fondest memory of us as kids. Oftentimes, Mama would put a blanket out on the grass for us so I could play with my dolls while Amir snuck out through the bushes to the nearest store to ask for chocolate. After a while, Mama caught on to his adventures, especially once she had a chocolate tab waiting for her that she knew nothing about! From then on, every time we played in the yard, Mama would tie a rope around my brother's waist and the telephone pole, giving him just enough room to roam around. Though it didn't take him long to maneuver his way out of the rope and escape once again.

As a child, I would hardly talk—to the extent that my mom worried I would never break out of that phase. Her neighbor told her an old wives' tale: if you feed your child a piece of bread from a poor traveler's bag, the child should break the pattern of speechlessness. I am still unsure how much that story had anything to do with me starting to talk, but my mom always reminds me that, after I ate the piece of bread, she obtained for me, I never *stopped* talking. My mouth often got me in trouble. After I discovered the power of speech, I would invite my mom's friends over for coffee without notifying her of the incoming guests. I would take all the food out of the fridge and make a spread on the table. Mom would ask, "What are you doing?" and I would gleefully respond, "Oh, the ladies are coming over for coffee!" Although I caused Mama so much embarrassment, I really couldn't help myself. I just always loved entertaining others, even at four years old.

In front of our house, there used to be a boulder that Dad dug up during the construction of our new home. I used to climb it, using it as my stage to sing all my favorite songs from Lepa Brena and Dragana Mirković. Mama used to cut the bottom of my bright pink tights so I would look like the singers on TV. Tata even made me a fake microphone, cord and all.

Both of my parents come from a large family. My dad had a Bosnian mother and a Macedonian father. Grandfather Isa died before my parents married, and Grandma Fata I only remember from pictures. I was three when Grandma died; I only vaguely remember the funeral. Mom was holding me in her arms as we stood over Grandma's casket to say goodbye. Grandma and Grandpa raised ten children together, six boys and four girls. Family visits on my dad's side were never dull. I spent much of my time playing with my cousins at our fun, lively family cookouts and parties.

Some of Dad's family lived in our village. Right next door, my father's Aunt Nazifa and Uncle Alija lived with their children, Belma and Amel—who, luckily, were about the same age as my brother and I were. We always played together. Just down the street from our house stood the property where my father's sister and her husband used to stay when they came for a few months' visit. Most of my dad's relatives were scattered around across Germany, Switzerland, and Bosnia. Every time a family member would come from out of town, the entire family would get together for a big party. Lamb roasts were always a must; you could never go wrong with having a variety of beef and potato pies. But my favorite? *Ćevapi* made on the grill with fresh pita and the traditional tomato-cucumber-onion salad with sour cream.

Happy Spirit

Grandpa Rašid and Grandma Esma had six children: three boys and three girls. Mom, the youngest of all, was born and raised in Kakanj, Bosnia. I loved visiting my grandparents, especially as they were the only ones I had growing up. To this day, I can still picture their big front doors, which were painted in a beautiful bright green color that represented our religion, Islam. My grandfather was a religious man and an *Imam*, a leader of the Mosque in the Zagradje community. This village was in the municipality of Kakanj, outside of the city. Grandfather was always a warm, loving, and straightforward man. There wasn't a safer or more comforting place than the security of his hugs. During my visits, we would hang out on the living room floor and listen to the news and music on the radio. I loved waking up to the static and muffled music of that old, beat-up box.

Grandpa was good man with a troubled past; he made certain decisions in life that haunted him until his death. His wealthy past caused constant conflict with most of the neighbors in the village. Fighting with words had never been his strong suit, and his stubborn will prevented him from resolving these issues. One tragic day, these traits sent him to jail for assaulting a neighbor. The altercation erupted over the damage of his land, caused by the neighbor's stupid cows. Rumors spread like wildfire. Was it self-defense, or was it something else? Not many were surprised with the outcome of the fight, considering that Grandpa had, allegedly, wanted to throw my mother off the city bridge the day she was born. How is *that* for a dysfunctional family? Mom's older sister saved her from that fate—or, at least, that's the story that I had been told growing up.

This WWII veteran left his family behind when he was sentenced to jail due to his poor choices. Grandma was regularly bullied by the neighbors for the actions of her husband, even though she was not at fault. Being all alone, she never opened the doors for anyone during that time. In my visits afterward, we spent most of our time together just hiding away from the prying eyes. I didn't see my grandfather for a long time after that, and the family never talked too much about it, either.

The drive up to my grandparents' house was one of my favorite pastimes with my family. I miss those simple moments with no worries as Mama and I sang along in the car to all our favorite songs. I loved the house my grandparents lived in, too; it was my favorite place to visit as a kid. I used to think of it as a faraway kingdom. There was always so much to do, so much to explore!

Family always gathered in the courtyard while Grandma cooked one of her pies. We spent most summers in the outside kitchen that had been built as an attachment to the summer den. It held yet another wood-burning stove and floor seating with cushions and pillows. We passed long warm days there, eating wild strawberries and grilling wild mushrooms. A wide stairway along the main house led to the backyard with a stretched-out hill and a garden at the bottom. This is where Grandma grew her own vegetables. We picked cherries during the summer and apples and pears in the fall; these were stored in the cellar at the bottom of the house. We loved running up and down the hill to play, stopping only when our stomachaches from eating too much fruit compelled us to fall asleep in the shade under the tree.

Of all these wonders, my favorite place in the house was Grandfather's study. He kept most of his treasures in there, but the most unique treasure of all was the water well that was right in the middle of the room. To me, this was the closest thing to a magical wishing well my young mind could imagine. Every time I drank the ice-cold water, I always made a wish.

My second-favorite place was the two-story barn. The upstairs held the animals' hay and food, and the downstairs held the cows and the horses. My grandparents also raised chickens and sheep. Many times, Amir and I would play hide-and-seek or jump around in the hay. We used to take the sheep up to the hill with other kids from the neighborhood. From the top, you could see my grandparents' house. We used to yell out to them, "Nano! Dedo!" as we roamed the top of the hill; they'd always wave back while they sat out in the courtyard. While the sheep ate the grass in the fields, we would pick more wild strawberries, blackberries, red currant, and mushrooms.

Half-an-hour's travel outside the village, my grandparents had a piece of land. We used to take day trips up there to collect hay for the animals. I rode on the horse with Grandpa or in the wicker basket, called *Samar*, while my uncle carried it on his back. I fell asleep easily in those baskets. They owned a small cottage with a barn on the lower level. During lunch breaks, we would go to the creek with a waterfall across the path to cool off on hot summer days.

I spent additional time at my grandparents' while my parents were building our new home. During the wintertime, we would gather on the floor of the main house, eating roasted chestnuts and pumpkin seeds. Grandma used to keep these perfectly round black stones up on the stove. After they warmed up, she would put them in a towel for me to keep my feet warm. The wood-burning stoves were popular back then; they were the only way to heat a home during cold winter days. Thus, Grandma had one in almost every room. Next to one stove in the kitchen was a little window that opened into one of the bedrooms.

Grandma used to knock on the window to wake me up so we could go milk the cows in the early mornings; we always had fresh milk for breakfast. I will never forget the in-floor concrete sink—or how many dishes I washed there as a child.

I remember Grandma dyeing her hair with *kana,* also called *henna.* I kept begging her to do mine as well, and she did! I was delighted, but Mama's reaction to her beautiful blonde-haired girl's transition into a redhead was not quite the same. From the distance she thought I was wearing a hat, but when she saw me walking down the road with my uncle, she yelled out, "What did you do to my child?" To me, she shouted, "Your father is going to kill us both!"

When we returned home, my dad joked that he wanted to send me back to my grandparents' house. I ran away that day. While sobbing, I made it all the way to the bushes behind the house before my mom came to get me. They had just finished the first story of the house. From the outside, a tiny hallway led to the kitchen, which then led to a wonderfully open living room. The smell of freshly painted wood, white walls, large windows, and warm hardwood floors gave me a feeling of comfort. I can still picture that moment from twenty-eight years ago.

The first floor of the house was supposed to be a temporary fix: two more floors were to be built before the house was finished, which, unfortunately, never happened. With a long way to go in the construction process, things started to get harder: news broke out about a war in motion, the one they called an *internationally armed conflict*. Yugoslavia collapsed under the consequences of cultural controversy and economic struggle of the Serbian President at the time.

Bosnia's separation from Yugoslavia in 1992 brought a great deal of bloodshed to the country. The Serbian Armed Forces carried out what they called *ethnic cleansing*, killing thousands of people. Eighty percent of those men, woman, and children were Bosnian Muslims.

Our neighbors and friends started abandoning their homes, moving to safer parts of the region. We used to hide out in the basement of my aunt and uncle's house next door. We watched the news, and our president gave a speech about the fall of our country. We waited, anxious and fearful, for things to improve—or for a bomb to strike. Would it be a neighbor's home? A friend's? Ours? No one was prepared for what came next.

Noises

I woke up to cries of terror in the neighborhood. Far in the distance, sounds of gunshots and bombs echoed as we felt the vibrations of explosions in the ground below us. After many violent incidents in the region, the time came for us to leave our home. Mom, speaking calmly through her tears, instructed me to grab anything I could; I gathered some toys and a blanket (which I have kept to this day). Neighbors held their heads high to make sure they wouldn't be shot arbitrarily, while also watching the ground they walked on to avoid stepping on a mine.

Leaving our newly-built home also meant leaving my dad behind. He enlisted in the army to protect our home and our country. Military trucks arrived at the village to pick up everyone who was to be transferred to a safer location. Not many people stayed behind, and the ones who did would not have an easy life to look forward to. As we sat in the back of the truck that would take us away from our village, we were overwhelmed with the screams and moans of distress that could be heard throughout the entire neighborhood. I waved goodbye to my dad, not knowing if I would ever see him again. It isn't something any five-year-old should have to *imagine*, let alone experience. That day is carved deep into my memory.

My mother, brother, and I left our life behind, only to start a new one when we arrived at the refugee camp in a small village outside the city of Tešanj. Everyone received a number to their assigned room. As we settled in, we learned that we would be sharing our room with another family. In some way or other, everyone helped each other to the best of their abilities. Each family received a generic care package for survival, each filled with canned foods, toiletries, and the necessities needed to get by. The closest thing to candy we had was powdered milk, which was my favorite. A few houses down from the refugee camp, my dad's aunt and uncle, our neighbors from Orašje, stayed with another family. Luckily, we saw each other all the time. I don't recall the exact length of time we spent there, but it wasn't long before we had to keep moving again.

The Serbian Army had taken over our homes, so the only option left was to keep moving, to keep running. Outnumbered and vulnerable, we learned to do everything silently without bringing any attention to ourselves or our loved ones. As the war grew worse, so did the community ties that once stood united and solid. Some people stopped trusting and only kept to themselves. We soon learned that everything had a cost, and people became greedy during the war.

From the refugee camp in Tešanj, we went on to stay with my mother's sister, Aunt Ramiza. I always loved the view of her house as we walked towards it. My aunt and her family lived on a farm in a village called Bradići outside the city of Maglaj. My favorite part of the visit was watching the trains go by from her living room window. I used to run outside and wave excitedly to the strangers. Once the war broke out, though, not many people traveled anywhere. For a long time, the trains passed, but they remained empty.

Like my grandparents, my aunt and uncle had

animals too. Cows and chickens were their livelihood. They sold eggs, milk, homemade cheese, and other dairy products to the neighborhoods. Across the yard, after the train tracks and the cornfield, and past the main road was a river we used to swim in, *River Bosnia*. In the river named after our beautiful country, my cousins, Amir, and I would swim against the current on hot summer days, racing to see who could swim faster. Part of my childhood will always be there, the part I carry in my heart.

Many of my family members refused to leave their homes during the war; because of this, they suffered much more than I did. There is a certain pride in building something with your own hands, and many homes in Bosnia were built by their owners from ground up. Something so special is not so easy to leave behind.

As the days passed by, our living situations worsened, and the war became more terrifying. We packed up again, and this time we were on our way to Switzerland. Buildings and landscapes were no longer beautiful; tragedy struck in the form of sad, deteriorating walls and broken windows. The destruction of our homes was chilling. Our country was falling apart. Far in the distance, the houses were no longer visible. Black smoke that traveled through the sky had collected in the air above the roofs of our beaten-up shelters. We decided moving forward was the only way in hopes of a brighter future.

I have very few memories of living in Switzerland. We stayed with my aunt's family. My father's sister was a strict and intimidating woman; we were never able to put *anything* past her. All the food on my plate had to be gone before I got up from my seat, the fridge was not allowed to be opened without asking permission, and daily naps were a rule. Despite this, she did take us on the trips to the lake, and Amir and I were permitted to attend kindergarten with our cousin. We weren't registered—it was more like a visit, but it made us feel like we were experiencing part of a real childhood. Another of my father's sisters used to take us to the zoo to see all the animals. I remember visiting my uncle's house often. He even gifted me a Minnie Mouse snow globe: a rare, prized possession for a displaced child. I held on to that piece of treasure for twenty years—until it fell and shattered a few years back.

Everything was more complicated during the war, and it became a lot harder to accomplish certain things, things necessary for survival. Only two months after we moved to Switzerland, we were forced to leave *again*. We were refused a fighting chance to start over and live a peaceful life. Our options were limited: go home to a war or immigrate to Slovenia. My uncle had lived in Slovenia most of his adult life and offered to take us in.

We drove for a few hours before reaching the border with hopes that things were about to get better. We got through the Switzerland-Austrian border with no problem and drove all the way through Austria without any trouble. At the Slovenian border, however, we didn't have as much luck. They did not let us into the country. We were stuck and there was nowhere left to go, no place to call home. I felt that nothing could be scarier. We were a miserable sight: a twenty-five-year-old mother, a five-year-old daughter, and a three-year-old son. Amir wouldn't stop crying, I kept getting a bloody nose from the heat, and my mom was barely holding back the tears, being strong for all three of us. We spent all day sitting in the hot sun, just waiting.

Finally, a woman that worked in the restaurant at the border approached us, and asked if we needed help. She had seen us sitting there while she was taking a break. She talked to my mom for a little, and then walked away. After maybe half an hour, she came back with food, water, some sunglasses, and other toys to entertain Amir and me.

The sun finally set, the chilly night came, and still we were waiting outside. A border patrol officer approached us and asked if we would like to come inside where it was a little bit warmer. He was a sweet man; it was thanks to him that I tried doughnuts for the first time. Our new friend did not rest until he made sure we got through the border. He reached out to my uncle and told him where to meet us so we could get home safely. My family was being taken care of by another human being. This man had no connection to us or any obligation to help, yet he showed compassion to a young mother with two small children. He made sure we were safe and that we arrived at our destination. This day, now so long ago, taught me to never underestimate how a small amount of kindness can go a long way—or even mean *everything* to someone. You never know what anyone is going through, regardless of the struggle, the kindness you show can change a person's life in only a positive way.

My uncle waited for us across the street at a bar while we crossed the border, and after all the madness, we finally made it to our new home. As I fell asleep next to my brother, all the troubles of the day started to fade away. I slowly drifted off into slumber. I felt that perhaps *this* new start would finally be my chance to have a childhood, to live my life in peace with my family—but struggle came with every change. I, once again, had to adjust to a new home, a foreign language, and the task of making new friends.

CHAPTER TWO

Unfamiliar

We lived with my uncle in a little apartment on the other side of Kidričevo's train station. I took in the view of the exterior orange walls of the one-bedroom apartment next to the bright yellow walls of an old train station bar. Mom worked here for a while, cleaning to earn some money. Across the street was the front yard, a rustic wooden shed with chickens and goats, and stretched-out grassy fields where we grew our own vegetables. Amir and I were eager to pass the days playing in the yard.

Susjed and Susjeda, our next-door neighbors, were an older couple who lived in an apartment attached to the old train station storage building. We spent a lot of time with them. During Christmas, they would let us come over to see their Christmas tree. I had seen Christmas trees before in passing—I had sat on Santa's lap once back home, even receiving a *paketić,* or goodie bag—but some of those memories were ones I could only recall from pictures. Experiencing it in real life was something quite special for me. I used to pretend I lived in the Christmas village under the magical Christmas tree.

As a Muslim family, we hadn't grown up celebrating Christmas. Perhaps it wasn't ours to celebrate, but we still found it fascinating and beautiful. If you ask any of my friends, they can tell you that my absolute love for the holiday persists to this day. Mom let us have a tree—more for New Year's than Christmas—but, to me, it still held a special meaning because it felt like *magic.* I used to make paper snowflakes, ornaments out of aluminum foil (so they would be shiny like the ones on TV), and garlands of paper-link chains. Even with the turmoil happening in the world and all we had lost, being a kid back then definitely had its extraordinary moments.

I loved celebrating December 6th: St. Nicholas Day. The Feast of Saint Nick was a special day of gift-giving for the children. On the eve of the holiday, each child would place a shoe on the windowsill outside before bedtime in hopes that, by morning, the shoe would be filled with treasures. The next day, we would run outside to find the shoes overflowing with candy, different baked goods, chocolate gold coins, and toys too. We spent our winter breaks playing on the abandoned trains behind the train station. We explored those trains from corner to corner, climbed all the way to the top, and saw the entire village from there. It used to snow enough for the plows to create giant piles. Amir and I would take our sleds, climb to the top, and slide down the snowy hill all day long. On the way home, we'd stop at our friends' house next door for cookies and hot cocoa.

We spent our summer at the public pool or visiting my uncle at work. He helped us build a secret fortress with some boxes, and we played in it day-in and day-out. The best kind of memories of my childhood are the ones in which I spent exploring the immense world of my imagination. Everything is so much *bigger* when you are a child. Now, when I look back on some of the pictures, I can't believe how small everything was—but, to this day my imagination remains immense. I never went to preschool or kindergarten. Mom kept putting school off in hopes that conditions would improve, that we could return home soon, but the war got even worse. In September of 1993, when I was seven years old, I started first grade.

The first day of school was scary and exciting at the same time. Mama and Amir took pictures with me that morning. I remember wearing a bright blue and green backpack that didn't match anything at all, a purple sweater, and a black mini-skirt with, of course, some black tights. I went to Boris Kidrič Elementary School. I would walk to school by myself—I took a certain route every day—and I always loved the way that the morning sun shined its warmth on my face. The first few months of school were terrifying. Because I did not speak the language, I had no friends. Because I had no friends, I was bullied. These were a lot of changes for one kid to go through all at once. Eventually, the circumstances got better. My first-grade teacher helped me through; she even wrote a letter to my mom so she wouldn't worry about me adjusting. I still have that letter somewhere. All it took was a little patience and positivity, even when everything around me felt negative. I started making friends, and I loved them so much.

There was one girl I remember. Her name was Adriana, and she lived with her family in an apartment building down the street from our school. We were inseparable: we walked home from school together, played on the weekends, spent our birthdays together, went to the nearby park, and even got head lice from one of the girls in our classroom. I hated the smell of the shampoo Mama used to get the damn critters out, but at least Adriana and I both got to stay home from school.

I remember Halloween in Slovenia a little *too* well. We sat on the floor of Adriana's living room and terrorized ourselves with scary movies. That was the first time I saw *Edward Scissorhands*. All the refugees would gather to walk around town in our white dove costumes, which represented peace. The excitement—and even the fear—I felt from the holiday meant I was *finally* having a normal childhood. These were the good days. As much as I wish I didn't remember some of the dark ones, you can't have only the good without the bad.

No matter what I endured as a child, Mama had always been there to comfort me in the way only a mother can. I once became sick enough to spend two weeks in the hospital, where she visited me every day. I looked forward to seeing her—and to all the snacks she used to bring me. There was lots of PEZ candy!

Then, Mama made new friends, some closer than others. I don't know for certain how she was feeling at that time, but I do remember how I felt. I missed the familiar comforts of a mother, father, brother, and sister all united under one roof. As an adult, I now understand that promises can be broken, that nearly everyone has lied or deceived during a difficult time. I look back and realize that I have learned to fight through pain instead of masking it, to do everything in my power not to take the easy way out. I now believe that *you grow through what you go through.*

During my stay in Kidričevo, I had the wonderful opportunity to visit Italy. The Institution for Immigration offered a program that allowed refugee kids the opportunity of a lifetime. We travelled to the beautiful city of Rome, learning and experiencing a little of the good life outside of all the grief we had endured. This trip gave our parents the ability to go to work without worrying about their children. We got to be kids: to explore life and escape the real world.

Italia

I first visited Italy in the Summer of 1994. The seven-hour drive from Slovenia to Fiumicino was one of the best road trips I had ever been on. Laughter and chatter took over the entire bus as we envisioned the new adventures awaiting all of us. Each kid received a coloring book and a dictionary to pass the time during the drive. We were taught basic Italian words and familiarized ourselves with some of the Rome's most famous places, like the Colosseum and the Trevi Fountain. Driving through the city was like traveling to a whole new world; it was like nothing we had ever experienced before. I felt energized by the morning sun shining through the window, by the feeling of everything to come in the next few weeks, and by the promise of adventures to share with a new friend. Elvira, my buddy on the bus, was also assigned to be my roommate at the Cavalli residence.

When we arrived in Fiumicino, our bus pulled into a grand plaza where our host families waited for us. As soon as I got off the bus, I heard my name being called from the crowd by the people who would be my family for the summer. This is when I met Paola and Fabrizio for the first time. I would come to know them as some of the most caring and wonderful people I had known. To my brother and me, they were like second parents. The love and compassion I received from them has no comparison; they took me in their arms and into their home as if I was their own child.

To a seven-year-old, arriving at their house was like arriving at a castle. I explored every corner of Paola and Fabrizio's home that summer. They introduced me to *Un Posto Al Sole*, their restaurant, where I ate all the spaghetti and pizza I wanted. I half-jokingly considered the statue at the front entrance to be my boyfriend, mostly because "he" was as tall as I was. They took me to the concert venue where I practiced my dance moves with Paola's sisters, Antonella and Simonetta, and listened to the live bands on the weekends. On hot days, we cooled off in the pool where Paola and Fabrizio taught me how to swim; I spent hours in the water. Every day after lunch, we would hang out by the pool. There was a plastic rock that covered the pool mechanics. For some reason, I *loved* sitting on that rock and pretending I was the Little Mermaid. I also loved getting dressed up for dinner—and, although we weren't *technically* allowed to eat it before supper, Elvira and I spent countless hours stealing gelato out of the fridge and letting our friendship blossom.

In Italy, I was given the opportunity to experience a childhood that my parents could not offer me at that time. Paola and Fabrizio, along with the rest of the family, always took us on wonderful adventures around Rome. Every day was a new experience with the Cavalli family. Our days at the local amusement parks flew by in flashes of roller coasters, princess carriage rides, and carousels. I lived every child's summer dream.

Paola would take Elvira and me, along with the girl from next door, to the ranch to ride horses. Sometimes, we'd sit on a bench for hours, eating our ice cream while we watched Paola masterfully ride her horse. Roller skating was also a major part of the Cavalli family's summer schedule, as all the sisters competed in roller skating tournaments. We visited

Fabrizio's store often. I was even gifted a little floral treasure box that I have kept to this day. It's the little things that hold the most sentimental memories.

I reveled in even the simplest of adventures: just riding in the car, looking out the window, and chewing *a lot* of bubble gum. The smell of it always reminds me of Italy. Our adventure took us over to visit the girls' aunt. She had an Indian blackbird called Giggio. I always tried to get him to talk, because I thought he should, like a parrot!

Throughout all these strange and wonderful new adventures, the one I recall as the most eye-opening had to be the first day we went to the airport. I rode the escalators up and down and caught my first sight of a plane taking off into the sky. I remember feeling that I hadn't seen anything like this in all the world before. I was overcome with a sense of *magic*, and the seeds were first planted for my love of travel. Even now, hardly anything can match the thrilling feeling I find in airports and while flying. Each time I travel, I rediscover that sense of anticipation, of adventure; I crave the experience of discovering the world all over again.

The organization that brought us to Italy hosted many parties for us. All the kids from the refugee camps got to reconnect for the day and brag about who had the best family. I wouldn't have traded my host family for a mine of gold; I would not back down from my opinion that they were the best. This is one of the reasons why I can't wait to have a family of my own one day. Perhaps my life up until now hasn't played out quite the way I dreamed it would, but maybe—just maybe—having my own family could be my ultimate second chance to do the things the right way. I dream of giving the love I feel I needed as a child when my family was struggling, and the world was crumbling around me. I dream of giving the love I felt from the people who took it upon themselves to give me—and the other refugee children—a chance to explore the world and forge happy memories.

Before we knew it, the trip—and all the fun that came along with it—was at its end. We had to return home. When I got back to Kidričevo, I remember Mama unpacking my suitcase and asking where all my clothes had gone! By the end of the summer, my suitcase consisted mostly of toys that Paola and

Fabrizio had bought me.

The months passed by, but there still hadn't been a day that I didn't think of my friends back in Italy. I missed them so much! One day, Mama told me that she had received word that my friends were coming for a visit. It was almost Christmas, and I spent the entire day looking out the window. I waited and waited for them, but they never showed up. Heartbroken, I cried myself to sleep. The next day, I went to school for my last day before the winter break started, assuming they had forgotten about me and that I would never see them again. On the way back from school, I met my mom halfway; she said she wanted to take me to the bakery to cheer me up. Chocolate doughnuts, of course, always helped.

A child with a broken heart can seem inconsolable, but that all changed when we arrived back home. Think of a time that someone has done something extraordinary that made you feel incredible, important, loved, and wanted: that's how I felt mere moments later. As soon as I walked into the house, my dear friends from Italy ran out, yelling, "Surprise!" I was caught up in an amazing moment that will forever be a wonderful memory. I couldn't stop crying, but these were now happy tears. Their trip didn't just consist of a visit; my friends had come to take me back with them. Best news ever!

That winter, I spent Christmas in Italy, decorating the tree and opening wonderful presents. I remember that time as the most magical Christmas a child can experience; they gave me that. Early in my visit, I eyed up a pink musical carousel and a green light-up toy watch. I thought of how *badly* I wanted them as we shopped in the plaza. On Christmas Eve, Santa himself gave them to me! Excitedly, I called my mom to tell her about all my new gifts. I used to pull up a chair next to the payphone on the wall, climb up, and call Mama every day to keep her up-to-date on all my exciting adventures. The magic of that winter remains fresh in my memories, but, time marched forward.

After I finished second grade, Mama, Amir, and I had to move again. After two years in Kidričevo, we were headed to a refugee camp. Once again, we were travelling toward a new home, a new school, and new friends.

United

Our new adventure took us forty-five minutes outside Kidričevo and into the suburbs of Ptuj. It was not the farthest we had travelled, but it was far enough away to ensure that we'd be starting over once more. This time around, I was fortunate enough to find some familiar faces in the refugee camp; I knew some of the kids from the bus to Italy the summer prior. Refugees from different parts of Bosnia, Croatia, and Serbia came together in the hopes of creating a somewhat peaceful life.

It had been almost three years since the war had started and we had left our home. Unfortunately, not long after, another tragedy struck. The Srebrenica massacre killed over eight thousand people at the hands of the Serbian army, which was under the command of the Bosnian-Serb General who would later be convicted for crimes against humanity.

Everyone had hoped for a chance to move back home, but these unfortunate events kept us away. The war wouldn't end until December 1995.

At that point, it had been such a long time since I had seen my father. He had come to visit us while we lived in Kidričevo, but he always returned to the battlefield. One day, we received news that Dad had been admitted to a hospital in Switzerland. The message indicated that he had been shot in the leg and dismissed from his war duties.

Rumors spread about the war coming to an end, but no one knew for sure. Everyone had grown accustomed to our new way of living: what we considered the *safe* way. Although, even years later, people would remain afraid to go back, our fear had a purpose. It helped us to grow stronger and braver and helped us overcome the harsh conditions that were our reality.

The refugee camps in Ptuj were hosted in a long, narrow, wooden, one-story barracks. We had a main dining room hall with a kitchen for everyone to share. We all used to eat together during the holidays, which were a mix of old and new traditions. We colored eggs during Easter, decorated for Christmas, made desserts and pastries during Eid Mubarak, and enjoyed movie nights. The religious divide didn't exist here like it did before the war—or like the way that it exists today; people showed kindness to one another and took good care of each other.

We had communal bathrooms and showers, and many families shared rooms as well. I can still picture the beat-up walls of the room in which we lived. I was lucky enough to have my own bed this time, and Amir slept next to Mom on the other bed. We shared this single room with another family for the first few months, but they ended up moving back to their village. We had the entire room for ourselves!

Our living arrangement was very different this time around, but everyone was in the same situation; no one had it better than any other. Bosnians, Croatians, and Serbs, each with a different religion and different cultures, worked together. Even though our people were battling each other back home, we looked past our differences and got along at the camp. Everyone looked forward to the future, whatever we imagined it might be at that time.

On summertime weekends, we'd go to the park down the street from the refugee camp for picnics and bike rides. It needed a bit of work, but that was part of its charm. It hosted a rundown building that vaguely resembled a castle and lent the park an air of mystery.

We spent many hours in the park with our families—and the volunteers from Italy. All of us children would delight in the help (and the many gifts) the volunteers brought. Our favorite part was playing games, such as the parachute game, scavenger hunt, and hide-and-seek. We gathered in pairs and played hand-clapping games while singing Italian songs, such as "La canzone della felicita" and "Michizuele." The volunteers even set up a mini-zipline! I'm always overcome with a sense of nostalgia—and a bit of sadness—when I see an empty park; it seems that kids today are missing out on the unbridled joy of passing the afternoon outdoors.

During our time in Ptuj, the camp organized many fun activities and trips to pass the time. Summer in Ptuj brought new and wonderful opportunity: We could once again visit our host families in Italy! This time, we traveled by airplane. It was my first ever ride in the craft that had captured my imagination, and my love for travel grew even stronger.

I felt the excitement and anticipation all over again as I was driving down *Via Passo Buole* to see my friends. They never ceased to amaze me—my room was ready for my arrival, filled with toys, clothes, and my favorite treats. When I first met Paola and Fabrizio, they had just gotten married. Each summer there, I'd watch their wedding video and fall in love with love, dreaming that one day, my wedding would be just as magical as theirs. I'd picture the beautiful Basilica, the gorgeous wedding gown, and my own Prince Charming standing next to me. Of course, I had smaller dreams, too. Paola had beautiful porcelain dolls sitting on her bed that I longed to play with, even though I wasn't supposed to touch them—but I'd use them to play out the stories from my imagination all the same.

Every time I visited, I always stayed in the second part of the house with Paola's sister, Antonella, and their grandma. Each morning, I would walk into the kitchen filled with sunshine and the crisp morning breeze, take my seat at the table, and relax while Nonna made me hot chocolate and warm pastries. After breakfast, I would wait on the terrace for Antonella until it was time for us to be off to our next adventure. The family hosted excellent pool parties and a lot of birthdays. Elvira and I got matching black-and-white polka dot dresses for one of the parties, and we even got to blow out candles on the cake!

The band still played in the concert hall on the weekends. I loved dancing to their music, and the band must have taken note: before I left that summer, they gave me one of their tapes so I could listen to them any time. A small arcade occupied a little nook by the entrance of the hall, and I spent hours playing games like Pac-Man, Mortal Kombat, and Street Fighter. I learned the Macarena in my old favorite restaurant; the girls that worked there taught me the moves while playing the tape on repeat. Most of all, I cherished the big family meals we always shared, whether at home or out at a restaurant. Everyone enjoyed each other's company and ate amazing food. After dinner, we would pick yellow plums off the trees in the yard for dessert.

The summer vacation was coming to an end. Once we returned to the refugee camp, I got ready to start third grade. For the first time ever, I walked to school with friends and didn't feel quite so alone. I became involved in many afterschool programs while attending classes there. I joined a dance team with all my friends, and we always put on shows for our visitors. We learned to work with one another as a team, to overcome our fears and insecurities, and to fend for ourselves while looking out for each other. I also learned to sew and cook (although only one took hold: today, my cooking is much better than my sewing ability).

I finished third grade in Ptuj in June of 1996; we hadn't even spent a full year there before we had to keep moving once again. The entire refugee camp was being torn down to build a factory. Late in the summer, we arrived at our new home: the refugee camp in Celje. Again, we went through the familiar routine of receiving our key and our care packages. This time, our room was roughly seventy-two square feet: it was like a tiny house for three people. It featured two twin beds that sat against the wall, a small window, an in-wall closet, a few shelves, and a little nook with a mini-fridge. There was a small TV mounted to the top left corner of the window above the bed. One night, as I was dozing off to sleep, I remember catching a snippet of *The Wizard of Oz* playing on the TV. It would be years later until I saw the movie in full, but I always remembered the brief glimpse of magic I caught that night. Mom slept on one bed, and Amir and I slept on the next, leaving us opposite each other.

Our building was surrounded by barracks and run-down huts that the refugee kids used to decorate with graffiti art. We drew with chalk everywhere we could. We played hopscotch and carved our names into the tree outside our new home, hoping to leave traces of ourselves. We played soccer in the field behind the building and hide-and-seek around the barracks. We took walks together to the library and to Sunday school. I resumed my studies again that fall; I was starting fourth grade at the Elementary School Lova in Celje.

All the while we lived in the refugee camps, we felt trapped in a pattern. Each camp was different, but there was never any movement forward. Parents worked to earn any living they could, and kids went to school or stayed home alone. I was ten by then, so I was always tasked with looking after Amir. The moments that stood out were any of those that broke the pattern.

One night, as Amir and I were sleeping, Mom woke us up with an awesome surprise. Tata had come for a visit, and he was doing much better since his injury! The visit was brief, though—my father had stopped by, only for a few hours, to tell us he was travelling back to Bosnia. He hoped to find a house where we could all live together again. Tata left the next afternoon. Late in the Spring of 1997, Mama began packing, and after school ended Amir and I would be heading to Italy for our summer trip with our friends. Every time we relocated, we traveled differently. This time it was by train: an amazing new experience!

That was the last time I saw my friends in Italy, and it's hard to believe that it has been over twenty years since then. I still hope I will someday find a way to see them again, if only to have a nice big plate of spaghetti once more with my second family.

CHAPTER THREE

Homecoming

The war was over; we could finally return to Bosnia and back to our roots. We made our new home in Jablanica, a village outside the city of Maglaj. We drove through the streets of this unfamiliar place, anxiously waiting to arrive at our new house. We pulled up the driveway of a beautiful two-story home as neighbors and loved ones from both sides of the family gathered around to welcome us. It felt like an unbelievable opportunity to see our friends, and family once again after all the years of being apart, and it was extremely gratifying. Happiness, laughter, and tears filled the air; everyone celebrated life in *peace*.

After dinner, Dad took us on the tour of the house and the outside garden. It had taken eleven years for me to have my own room, and Amir and I were both thrilled to have our own space. Four walls and a bed that I didn't have to share with *anyone* felt like heaven. Those four walls were certainly adorned with many posters over the years. Being the oldest, I was permitted the bigger room, which caused more than a few sibling fights—but what are brothers and sisters for if not to lovingly fight with each other? For the first time since we left Doboj in 1992, we didn't have to cook, sleep, and eat in the same room.

Mama had a gift for making any home comfortable and beautiful for us. It didn't matter if it was one room or an entire house: she knew how to decorate—and she loved her plants. There was one in every room of the house. In the living room alone, she dedicated an entire wall to plants. Tata built her a beautiful hanging wall shelf where she kept them all. Mama even put a plant in Amir's room, right on the side table, to brighten up the space a little. She couldn't figure out why it started drying out and dying, especially since she always made the effort to water it regularly. Later, she realized that Amir had been peeing in it—he explained that he was too scared to go to the bathroom downstairs in the dark! She never put another plant in his room.

I used to love spending mornings in my parents' room before school. The space would emit a beautiful, golden light as the sunshine reflected off the hardwood floors. Warm and cozy, I would lounge on the bed while Mom hung clean laundry out on the balcony. I felt like you could see almost *everything* from up there. During summertime, I would sit on the balcony and watch the night sky, catching a glimpse of the occasional shooting star. On weekend mornings, we would have breakfast consisting of *kifle and Pašteta argeta* (fresh bread sticks and chicken pate spread) on the lower balcony. Outside in the garden, there was a grape arbor with a swing underneath that Tata built for Amir and me. Mama did a lot of gardening too; she was a stay-at-home-mom for as long as I could remember. Although Tata was back in our lives, he would often travel for his construction work. He would be gone for two weeks at a time—and sometimes even longer.

Our house faced the main road, and behind us stood two additional houses. I was thrilled to learn of potential new friends who lived at the house at the end of the pathway, next to the abandoned building. A small creek, perfect for splashing around in when it got too hot, ran through the forest behind the building. Amela, Alma, and Izeta were the first friends I made when we moved back home. They lived with their grandma and their dad. We became friends instantly and spent the entire summer playing together. Amela was the oldest, Alma was the middle sister, and Izeta was my brother's age—they also went to school together. Amela introduced me to her best friend, Ilda. They had been friends since childhood and lived through the war together; once I came into the picture, the three of us were inseparable.

We always sat next to each other on the bus on the way to school and walked to Sunday school every weekend. We played "house" at the abandoned buildings across the street, used Amela's father's old van as one of our imaginary homes, and even pretended to be famous singers. On the weekends, we would gather at the elementary school across the street with the other kids. We used the staircase as our stage while the younger kids pretended to be the audience and cheered for us. I felt fortunate to have such an amazing group of friends to play with all the time.

We went through our rebellious stage together, too. We smoked cigarettes for the first time, stole corn from the farm across the street and cooked it on the open fire behind Amela's house, and snuck downtown without permission. We broke into the abandoned part of the school and created our own classroom so we could play as teachers.

During the hot summer days, we would hike up to the creek called *Markove Bare*, a manmade pond where we would all go swimming. A little further down the street was a beautiful waterfall; everyone would jump off it into the sinkhole below. We would bring picnic baskets and eat lunch on the grass field. Sometimes, we grilled; oftentimes we would lie out in the sun and play games.

I was now fourteen. As if being a teenager wasn't hard enough *already*, things began to change, and I started becoming a woman. My heart was ready to fall in love for the first time, and the butterflies took over. I fell for a sweet and handsome boy with the most beautiful blue eyes who lived in the village. The day he asked me to be his girlfriend seemed perfect, like a scene out of a movie.

The village Masque celebrated its grand opening with a fair. The day started off with a prayer, followed by a concert and performances from the local artists. Children and adults alike were delighted by the atmosphere of dancing, food, and carnival rides. The handsome young villager and I spent the entire day sitting on the field, holding hands, and talking for hours with the rest of our friends. I felt loved, safe, and happy. Back then, I might not *quite* have known what it meant to be in love, but our affection for each other was genuine in the special way that all young love is. That night, he asked me, charmingly, to be his girlfriend. I cared for him and loved him—and, somehow, I always will. As the first ones always do, he holds a very special place in my heart.

As I grew older and experienced different, more complicated relationships, I began to understand some of the dynamics of love that my parents learned—and sometimes suffered—through the years. Not all marriages are perfect. Sometimes, one person in the relationship must walk away for a lesson to be learned.

This happened to my parents when my mom left us one morning.

I stood in the kitchen, heartbroken. I was sobbing too hard for the words to break through my tears. Begging Mama not to forget us, I handed her a picture of my brother and me. I didn't understand every aspect of my parents' fights, but I knew I didn't want to lose either of them from my life. Despite their mistakes, they were still my parents. A few days later, Dad decided to try his luck at bringing Mama home. We traveled to Visoko, where Mama had gone to stay with her sister. We arrived the day of Cousin Almira's wedding. Kids weren't allowed to attend the party, so we stayed at the house with my aunt and my grandma. Amir and I played with the kids in the neighborhood. We took walks up the hill, played soccer, and explored the abandoned church that held a special kind of charm and mystery. The day after the wedding, my mom agreed to return home, so we continued as if nothing had ever happened. Each family sets its own definition of "normal," so we carried on with our adjusted definition.

There is always struggle in life, but without struggle there are no lessons. We can choose the path of learning—or we can choose the path of ignorance.

I associate Jablanica with *growth*: it was one of those places where I grew as a person, learned a lot about myself, and came to better understand the people in my life. No matter where you grow up, the middle school years are crucial ones, filled with rapid changes and new perspectives. Although my family had returned to the familiar comforts of my home country, I was not immune to growing pains.

We spent four years trying to renovate our old house in Orašje. We were shocked to learn that the people next door had been using our home as a barn for their pigs! There was a lot of work to be done before the house was a home again. We spent every weekend going to the old village to restore the house back to its glory, all in hopes of one day moving back. Now we had two homes, the old and the new. I didn't look forward to one day having to leave my friends again and change schools, but that seemed to be my pattern in life.

The best times in middle school were the moments I spent with my friends. Our school was divided into morning shifts and night shifts; we would complete two weeks of the former before shifting to the later, then back again. My best friends and I were in different homerooms, but, if we passed each other in the hallways, we would hand notes to one another to stay connected. Like any middle schoolers, my friends and I counted down the minutes until we could catch up over lunch breaks. If one of us suggested, "Let's go to Zulejha's for a grilled pita!" we'd walk to the family-owned restaurant nearby; otherwise, we'd head down the street to the bakery for freshly-made pastries. I always ordered one with Nutella or poppyseeds. Our simple routines were comforting against the backdrop of change.

After about five years in Maglaj, just when I had begun to set roots, my parents decided to move again. I didn't know then if I would *ever* be done moving from place to place, and I can't say that I know now.

New Adventures

We received news that the U.S. Embassy in Zagreb, Croatia was accepting refugees for interviews that could lead to an even better opportunity: to live in America. My parents, eager to take this chance, asked my uncle to send over paperwork for us to begin the process.

In life there are no shortcuts, and this was, by far, one of the longest rides.

This life-changing opportunity was not without its challenges; as I had already learned, **nothing worthwhile in life is easy.** For us to move forward, we had to be Croatian citizens, which we were not. The first step in our journey seemed to be a dead end. One night, my parents invited our neighbors over for dinner, and the topic of our current dilemma came up in conversation. Our neighbors were also refugees. During the war, however, they had been hosted by a family in Croatia, a family that would be able to expedite our process. We were introduced to our new friends, Anica and Jure, who soon invited us into their home and unwaveringly supported our dream of moving to America.

During the interview process, we learned that travel outside Croatia was not permitted. Our entire lives would be picked apart: the way we lived now, our history, where we lived during the war, how we survived, how much money we made, and *even if we suffered enough*. Most concerning to us though, was the travel ban, as breaking it would result in immediate dismissal of the entire family's applications.

The problem was this: although we had found a family to host us during interviews, we still resided in a different country, and the application process was a lengthy one. This was not something to be sorted out in a weekend, or even in a few weeks. Every time we crossed the border, we had to beg the border officers not to stamp our passports; one small stamp would prevent us from ever moving forward. Luckily, they agreed—but only for a price, and theirs was cash and booze. This felt to me, like irony at its best: that even after the war, those in a position of authority would prey upon the broken people fighting for a better life. These border officers were not interested in upholding the law for the law's sake; they were interested in their own gain. We were pulled over so many times at the border. The officers would take our passports and force us to wait for painfully long intervals, scaring us into thinking it was all over. My dad used to beg them on his hands and knees, asking them not to take this opportunity away from his children.

After a yearlong process of distressing road trips between Bosnia and Croatia and the following interviews, it was time to learn our fate. We waited, along with other families, to find out whether we were going to America. In that moment, I felt like time was passing in slow motion. My head was spinning. My trance broke as I saw everyone jumping and crying. I broke out in tears, both happy and sad, as I realized that our names had been called. On one hand, I knew we were moving, yet again, from everything and everyone I grew to love; on the other, I couldn't help but imagine all the possibilities awaiting me in a brand-new world.

We returned home from the interview to one celebration after the next. We shared the news with our friends and family and slowly started selling all our belongings, as there were only so many items, we could bring with us. It was bittersweet. Leaving everyone behind was heartbreaking, but dreams of all the amazing things waiting for me eased some of the pain. Our family came around for goodbyes and farewells.

The night before we left, Amir and I gathered our friends and left for the city for one last time. We spent some time at Sultan, our favorite coffee place. Then, we walked around the city for a long time and took as many mental pictures as possible. By our ten o'clock curfew, we had returned home to continue our celebration. Mom and Dad went to the neighbors' house to say goodbye, but we stayed behind in a now-empty house with our friends. It felt so cold and bare that even the half-bottle of brandy Tata had gifted us for the occasion could not warm the room. We just sat around the table thinking: about memories, about changes. We cried, we laughed, we danced, and we reminisced. We recounted stories of all the times we had spent together, and then we cried some more.

The next morning, Mama woke me up to come downstairs for breakfast. Most of the family had arrived early to spend a little extra time with us. The neighbors brought food to share as our last meal in Bosnia. With only a few hours left, my friends met me by the abandoned post office across the street. We sat there on the grass and cried; my chest hurt so badly that it was as if someone was pulling on my heartstrings. Uncle Ferid picked us up, and soon we were on our way to Zagreb to spend the night at Anica and Jure's home. On our way, I remember driving by a house that was under construction. My former boyfriend was busy helping his dad, but I wished so badly I could have said goodbye in person.

Early in the morning on July 24th, 2001, we arrived at the Zagreb Airport. Along with the other refugees who had qualified, we were on our way to the United States of America.

America

Moving to the United States of America was nothing short of amazing. It was a dream come true and one of the greatest, once-in-a-lifetime opportunities that has ever happened to me and my family. As a young girl, I always had wondered what it would be like to live in a place like America. I grew up watching programs about the United States on television, hearing stories on the radio, reading magazines articles, and dreaming of what it would be like for me to experience this in person.

On the evening of July 24th, 2001, we landed at the Buffalo International Airport. After a thirteen-hour trip, we finally made it. I remember how overwhelmed I felt walking through the airport; it was the first time in my life that I saw so many different people. I had never seen a Hispanic person, an Asian person, or an African-American person before. Despite the initial culture shock, I was excited to experience more. We made our way to the baggage claim where my uncle waited for us.

The night air smelled sweet as a cool summer breeze brushed up against my face. I remember us driving down Kensington Expressway, what I now call the 33. I closed my eyes for a split second and felt such relief. It was a sense of peace, like I had finally made it *home*. I had lived many places before, but none of them felt like this. After moving around so much my entire life, I hadn't given myself permission to fully settle in before. This time felt different though. This time, America really was my home. As we pulled up to the house where my uncle lived with his family, the neighbors gathered around to welcome us.

For the first few weeks, we stayed with Uncle Osman, Aunt Edita, and Cousin Ena at their apartment in Buffalo. Everything happened so fast: we found a place to live, my parents applied for jobs, and my brother and I registered for school. We moved into a two-bedroom apartment in Cheektowaga. Mama got a job at Niagara Chocolates, and Dad did construction for the apartment complex where we lived. Every experience was new: there were unlimited things to try and places to go! My aunt and uncle took us to Darien Lake to ride the roller coasters, and we took several trips to Niagara Falls.

Just as family meals had shaped my experience in Italy, the food has always been my favorite part about moving to America. My first splurges were on pizza and Kit Kats. I indulged in drinking pop for breakfast regularly; back home, we drank water or milk, as pop was reserved for special occasions. My first trips to McDonald's and Burger King felt like stumbling upon a treasure chest, and discovering tacos was a very emotional experience for me. Food played a major role in my cultural transition, and I am not ashamed to say I became a bit of a glutton. Fast food was not readily available back home, so it was particularly thrilling throughout my first years in America.

That first summer, Amir and I spent a lot of time just walking around and exploring. Neither one of us spoke English, so we used the nearest library to our advantage. We rented books and movies and tried to learn as much as possible, especially since the new schoolyear was quickly approaching. We were motivated—but we were still teenagers enjoying our first American summer, so we spent almost as much time at the Cheektowaga Public Swimming Pool next to the library as we did explore.

Even before we moved to America, just like any teenager, I had spent my time obsessing over the Backstreet Boys, N*SYNC, and Brittney Spears; this passion continued in my new home. Jennifer Lopez was my all-time favorite; I listened to her second album on repeat, particularly focusing on my favorite song, "Ain't it Funny." I adored her Gypsy-style costume in the music video and was enthralled by her beauty. She quickly became a role model for my teenage years. I watched *7th Heaven*, *Roswell*, *Baywatch*, and *S Club 7* on television. I fell in love with Christmas movies, such as *Home Alone*, *A Christmas Story*, and *Miracle on 34th Street*. *Coming to America with Eddy Murphy* was on TV every weekend, and we had movie nights as a family. I spent countless hours pining over Leonardo DiCaprio and his character Jack, from *Titanic*; I hope I was not the only girl to tape a poster of him to my pillow that summer! Mama noticed my adoration of that beautiful young man and bought me a wristwatch at a flea market, with a picture of Jack and Rose in the background. I sang "My Heart Will Go On" for anyone who would listen, even though my rendition was not quite as powerful as the recording from the movie. How easy it was to fall in love with the world when I was younger!

We signed up for school: middle school for Amir and high school for me, both in the Maryvale School District in Cheektowaga, NY. I will never forget School Orientation Day. I was nervous and scared and armed only with the English phrases my brother and I had taught ourselves from the library and entertainment media. I didn't know what to do, who to talk to, or even where I needed to go! I did make one friend that day. She attended the orientation with her mom, and they helped me enormously. She spent the entire orientation with me and showed me where all my classes would be so I would be ready for my first day. We took a tour of the entire school to familiarize ourselves with the hallways, classrooms, and common areas.

Schools back home were *very* different. Before moving to America, I had never eaten in an actual school cafeteria; we were accustomed to running across the street to grab a sandwich on our half-hour break from classes. The first day of high school, I somehow managed to make it to my homeroom and take my seat. I remember feeling lost and intimated by everything—and everyone—around me. When everyone stood up to recite the Pledge of Allegiance, I was baffled. After the morning announcements, everyone went to their lockers to put their belongings away—everyone except me, that is. I returned to homeroom, still carrying my backpack, because I couldn't figure out how to open my locker. My homeroom teacher ended up asking one of the students help me out. Having someone help me transition, made a world of difference in the first few months of high school.

CHAPTER FOUR

Dazed

The first year-and-a-half of high school *terrified* me—especially after September 11th. I remember sitting in my art class as we watched the horrific announcement of the attacks on New York City on the news. My mom worried for Amir and me. Coming from a Muslim family put a target for judgement on our backs. I remember Mom calling and saying, "Please, don't tell anyone you are Muslim—and stay safe!" I didn't understand, at first, why we would be the ones held responsible; however, as I got older, I discovered it didn't matter if people knew your story. People stuck to their beliefs and judged, regardless. I never understood why: if one person from a certain culture or religion was bad, why did that person reflect on everyone else? To this day, I can still see the judgement and fear in people, despite who I really am, and it breaks my heart.

I spent most of my study halls in the designated ESL room doing my homework and reading. I struggled with the language, my new surroundings, and making friends, just as I had so many times before. Through high school, I always sensed that I didn't belong, perhaps even more so than a typical teenager would. We were all adjusting to the new responsibilities and routines of high school, but it took me six months to learn enough of my new language to feel somewhat comfortable in my day-to-day schedule. I owe credit to my favorite shows at the time, *Smallville and Gilmore Girls,* for helping me acclimate much faster. Sometimes, I wish I had been more outgoing and ambitious in high school. Would things have turned out differently if I had been able to integrate myself earlier?

Just as I had treasured the time I spent with my dance troupe as a young girl, I considered the school dances to be one the best parts of high school. My first opportunity came at the Freshmen Night Out.

Although I often felt worlds apart from my peers, I had managed to develop a crush on a boy in my grade. A friend who knew of my pining attempted to help me bridge the gap by asking him to dance with me. Fear crept into my mind. What if he spoke to me and I didn't know how to respond? Before my friend even finished talking to him, I knew what I had to do I ran away.

Transitioning to high school in America was turning out to be such a different experience than it would have been if I had stayed in Bosnia. I did not feel fully comfortable until the end of my sophomore year. This is when I began to understand the culture, improved my English, and built more meaningful friendships. Like a typical high schooler, I finally had favorite classes, favorite teachers, and a group of friends to sit with for lunch every day. From there, everything started to fall into place the way I felt it was supposed to.

Our ESL teachers were always there for us, no matter what. They helped us with any difficult classes and pushed us in the right direction with our education. We would host parties for the ESL students: peers from Poland, Ukraine, China, and even Brazil. I was always in charge of making the invitations and flyers. I was also tasked with decorating the classroom, which suited me well. I made some pretty great friends from all over the world—we might not have stayed in touch, but they made an important impact on my life.

I will never forget my Social Studies teacher. She was always kind to me and to Amir; she knew how to talk to us in the way that was most helpful with our transition. I enjoyed studying art and science, but I particularly loved Spanish class.

When I was seven years old—around the time we lived in Slovenia—I started watching telenovelas with my mom after school. The first series I ever saw was *Rosa Salvaje*, but it wasn't until I encountered Fernando Colunga that I became truly enamored with the Spanish language. The romance, the drama, and the excitement that every episode brought had me daydreaming, as usual, about one day being the main character in a story in which a girl falls in love with a handsome boy. Mom and I watched countless telenovelas over the years.

When I started ninth grade at Maryvale, every

student was required to study a foreign language—that is, everyone except for me. In Bosnia, all the students studied German; that was the only option available. I had spent four years of lessons attempting to string together a basic German sentence, but I picked up a decent amount of Spanish simply from watching my favorite telenovelas. The Spanish language had already become such an important part of my life, so I signed up for Spanish class, despite the ability to opt out. I couldn't have known it then, but my love for the language I first heard on television would grow over the years, and I'd eventually feel confident enough, speaking it myself. I had already taken one step toward becoming who I am today, but there were still more steps I'd need to take to escape my comfort zone and experience as much of high school as possible.

By junior year, I had signed up for high school musicals, joined the school choir, and started playing tennis. Being on the tennis team was a fantastic high school experience. I vividly recall going to matches, dancing with the girls on the bus, and meeting so many new people. I valued the friendships I made through my extracurriculars—and, even though the intensity of high school friendships often fades with time, it's always a delight to run into an old teammate or club member, whether it be at the grocery store, out at a bar, or at a country concert.

Spirit Week was everyone's favorite, and it always led up to the main event: The Homecoming Dance. My parents, as we were still finding our footing in America, couldn't afford to buy me a dress. Generously, the school offered me one on loan. Although I regret my attempt at a fashionable hairstyle all these years later, I still felt like a princess in my borrowed purple gown.

Another memorable experience was the field trip I took to Cleveland, Ohio with the choir. We toured the Music Hall of Fame and performed at Cedar Point. I even won a giant stuffed red monkey playing one of the arcade games. The bus ride was an experience in itself; the excitement and chatter were contagious.

As high school came to an end, I wondered if my time there could have been a bit better—a bit more fulfilling—if my experience had gone differently; I suppose many of us do. What if I had known the language from the start? What if I had taken my classes a bit more seriously and opened myself up to more possibilities? Questions like these never stop the march of time though, and my high school journey ended. Prom and graduation, it seemed, were over even faster. I didn't feel quite ready to leave high school, as though perhaps there was more to be done and explored—but my next chapter started, whether I liked it or not.

For Amir, middle school and high school provided a much different experience. Being younger, he transitioned more easily. He quickly became popular; it seemed he was constantly surrounded by adoring friends. He was always a people person—we shared that in common—but I was a bit more closed off than he was during that time. Amir entered the seventh grade as I entered high school, and the pressures I faced felt more immense. While I was battling expectations of perfection, self-imposed or otherwise, he was finding his stride. Four years flew by, and, just as I was becoming comfortable myself, it was time to leave.

Change does not wait for anyone; it just comes. Sometimes it is planned out, but most of the time it sneaks up on us, and we just have to figure out how to handle it.

I found myself sobbing on my bedroom floor. I was in the midst of a panic attack I had caused myself on the morning of my college orientation, all because I didn't want to grow up yet. I was terrified to step into the semi-adulthood of college and part time jobs; I wasn't ready to leave my friends or for change to come so quickly after I finally had begun to feel settled.

Life has a habit of playing out any other way than you've imagined, though. In college, making new friends came easily, and I barely heard from the old ones from high school. As I adjusted to this new stage, I thought about how funny it is that things change so unexpectedly and so rapidly.

Growing Pains

I was accepted to Villa Maria College for Interior Design, which felt like a good fit for me. I had always loved decorating and rearranging furniture. Anywhere I went, I automatically scanned the room and restructured it in my mind, designing it the way I thought it should look. Tata was always building something, and Mama kept every one of our homes looking beautiful, so it made sense that I inherited my love for design from the both of them.

Despite my natural inclinations toward design, I can't say that I was a particularly good student. My grades were average; I wasn't likely to be found quietly studying, and I'd be perfectly content never taking another written test again. I didn't absorb much from my dry textbooks, but I was inclined to learn as much as I possibly could be taught hands-on. Wisdom is a product of age and experience, though, and we tend to appreciate things differently as we get older. These days, I love learning new things more than I ever did before; I am always looking for something interesting to study.

My parents, my brother, and I moved into our new house in September of 2005. Life seemed to be improving for all of us. I was a full-time college student and was hardly home. I started working part-time at a retail store while Amir enjoyed high school and my parents worked on renovating our home in their free time.

For the first two years of college, I went with the flow: things were good, and I was very happy with where I was at that point in life. There were few things I had to worry about—until my grades started to suffer and everything changed. Since I worked a part-time job and lived under my parents' roof, I was somewhat financially supported by them, and, like any young person, I felt that they held it over my head. I resented my lack of independence and envied my friends who had it. I was trying my best, yet I felt like I was being dragged a hundred steps back for every step forward I attempted to take.

My day-to-day life, for some reason, wasn't making me happy anymore; I felt like I merely *existed* and just did the things I felt obligated to do. I tried to figure out what I wanted to do with my life—how to move forward—but the answer wasn't clear. During this time, my parents were fighting regularly, and I felt caught in the middle. Amir began rebelling, and we all started keeping to ourselves. My life had never been *simple*, but I longed for the simpler times, the ones that at least made sense.

Depression lingered at the edge of every move I made, but I kept pushing through any way I knew how. When I needed a good cry, I just cried myself to sleep. In the midst of the darkness, I had one thing to look forward to: my citizenship test. I was working toward becoming a citizen of the United States of America. I studied every day—and realized I probably should have paid more attention in my U.S. History class.

In December 2007, I became a United States Citizen. Standing in the courtroom that day and reciting the Pledge of Allegiance transported me back to my first day of high school, reminding me how far I had come from the morning when I had no idea what it even *was*. It will always be one of my proudest moment. Becoming a United States Citizen and receiving a letter from the White House was an extremely important and emotional moment, that I will remember forever. The day was made all the better knowing that Dad stood next to me, sharing my experience.

Mom received hers not too long after; it was another proud moment for our family. Amir was supposed to become a citizen alongside Dad and me, but his rebellious stage had gotten the better of him. My brother had been arrested for shoplifting, but it wasn't the first time he and his friends had gotten into trouble. Due to his probation, he had to wait a few months before he could apply for his test again. One day, we received a letter explaining that my brother had broken the law and could not proceed at that time. My father asked me to translate the letter for him, but, out of loyalty to my brother, I lied about its contents.

A year after I received my citizenship, I traveled back home to Bosnia to visit family. I was twenty-two, and it had been seven years since I had moved to America. I was almost as excited to travel on my own as I was to be on vacation for three whole weeks. The trip from Washington to Munich was the least comfortable plane ride I could have imagined. Being stuck between a middle-aged man who couldn't stop snoring and an elderly woman who smelled like she bathed in her perfume didn't make for a comfortable international flight. I hardly slept and couldn't stop sneezing; thankfully, I had my *Twilight* books to keep me company. Again, I dreamed of love, but this time my obsession—shared by women of all ages—was with a seductive vampire or handsome werewolf. I am not ashamed to say I am an avid daydreamer.

Nostalgia

I finally landed in Sarajevo. Cousin Adnan, along with his wife and son, came to pick me up. Our destination was my grandparents' house, the one I had always adored. My grandma had lived alone for many years now, and my grandfather had passed away from a heart attack in 2003. Once again, I was treated to the wonderful drive up to the village that I found so comforting. Everything seemed different this time—there were new houses, and the roads were now paved—and something was missing. It was the noise, I realized. The village didn't seem as lively as it used to be when the children would play outside all day. The only thing that remained unchanged was my grandparents' house. Even the giant green door, worn down after all these years, still made me smile as I walked through.

It seemed like time stood still there; every single

aspect of this house remained as I remembered. It was almost *untouched*. Every pillow had the same pillowcase, the black stones still sat on top of the wood-burning stove, the old radio still played that static music, and Grandma still had the little green bowl where she kept the sugar for her coffee. I took in everything like a breath of fresh air. Grandma had just finished with her daily prayer; she made coffee and put food on the floor table, or *Sinija*. We talked for hours before driving to my aunt's house.

For most of my trip, I stayed with Aunt Ramiza and her family in Maglaj, the same village where I had spent so much time as a child. Driving up to the house, I was taken back to 1992; the smell of the train tracks lingering in the air made my childhood memories seem so *present*. It was exciting to see everyone once again! I immediately enlisted myself to help my cousin plan her wedding while planning to see my old friends. Beni decided to take me around the old city and show me all the new developments. Hours into our exploration, we headed to the mall for some dinner. As we walked down the hallway, we were interrupted by a voice. "I can't believe you are here!" said the figure. As I looked up, I noticed the baby-blue eyes that I had fallen for so many years ago: it was my childhood love! I couldn't move at that moment. He hugged me so tightly that I could hardly breathe; in that moment, I became my fourteen-year-old self and fell in love all over again.

My cousin called my friend, Ilda, and asked her to meet up for coffee. After she declined, Beni handed the phone to me. "I didn't travel all the way over here to *not* see you," I exclaimed, revealing my presence. She couldn't believe I was in town! She met us out right away. We spent hours talking and catching up. As we chatted, a man came up to me and asked, "Are you Mirela?" I recognized him right away. He had married my mother's friend, the girl whose family lived in Croatia with Anica and Jure, the saviors who helped us move to America after the war.

I filled as many hours of each day as I could with my long-lost friends—as much as the trip was meant to be a family reunion, reconnecting with my friends was my favorite part. We went to concerts, spent hours at coffee shops, reminisced about the old days, and laughed *so much* at how crazy we had been when we were kids. I was gifted with more moments to spend with my best friends from Bosnia. I visited Amela and her sisters in Jablanica one afternoon. We took a walk around the village, remembering the good old days.

As easy as it was for our friendships to fall back into a comfortable rhythm, there were simple moments in which I realized how much things had changed— how much *I* had changed. I remember ordering a glass of water at a restaurant, much to everyone's shock. Ordering tap water, while so natural in America, is just not a custom in Bosnia.

There is something so comforting about taking a trip into the past and remembering the simpler times: ones with no worries or problems, just constant joy. Just as much as I was reassured and reinvigorated by the familiar sights of home, I was also looking forward to the upcoming celebration of change. As the day of the wedding approached, the air was thick with energy; everyone ran around frantically to complete last-minute responsibilities. Finally, the day of the wedding arrived. Beni and I kept ourselves busy getting ready in her room with the rest of the girls while we watched out the window for the guests to arrive at her parents' home.

Bosnian wedding traditions are very different from the ones in America, and I was eager to experience them again. The hosts had set up the upper floor of the house with tables covered by white cotton tablecloths and old wooden chairs. Food was spread out like a hundred Thanksgiving dinners. The house was warmly heated by the fireplace, and yet there was a crisp breeze coming through the front door as all the guests walked in. As they arrived, one by one, my aunt pinned a decorative flower to the suit or dress of each guest: this tradition is called *Kićenje*. Music flowed through the old walls of the house as the accordionist played and sang his heart out. The guests grabbed each other by the hands and started moving in circles, dancing the traditional wheel dance called *Kolo*.

One of the girls and I teamed up to decorate the guests' cars with balloons, flowers, and bows. The vehicles lined up and down the dirt road all the way to the barn. Once we completed our duties, we snuck around the barn for a cigarette and some drinks. After about two hours of eating and drinking, the time came for the bride to come out of hiding and reveal herself to the guests. Everyone gathered outside the house; the swelling music heightened our anticipation. The bride arrived, walking outside with her two brothers on each side of her. As she reached the midway point of the stairs, we began the bartering, or "the buying of the bride." The groom's brother, who doubled as his best man, or *Kum*, made a payment to the bride's brothers in order to let her go. It is a Bosnian tradition for the groom's family or best man to "buy" the bride from her family; as the groom's side offers a payment, the bride's side either declines or accept the offer. As is the custom, the money goes to the bride's parents, who are responsible for paying for half of the wedding.

From the bride's house, everyone got into their decorated cars and drove down to City Hall. During the trip, each car drove slowly down the road and beeped their horns all the way to our destination, notifying the neighbors of the wedding celebration. Then, according to tradition, the young children locked hands to create a chain, preventing the cars from passing by. The wedding party and guests are obligated to toss them candy and coins in order to be permitted to pass. We threw the prizes out of our car windows, allowing us to continue to our destination. Once we arrived at City Hall, the bride and groom made their way to their seats with their *Kum* and *Kuma*. After the official marriage, singing and dancing broke out in the plaza, signaling the bride to throw her bouquet.

From there, we went to the Masque for the religious ceremony, followed by a party at the groom's house for the rest of the day's celebration. As we made our way up to the village where I once lived, I found myself overwhelmed with a wave of emotion, both good and bad. The wedding was like a reunion: the family, friends, and neighbors I hadn't seen in so long were all in attendance. It was bittersweet to feel such connection and belonging, all the while knowing I would be leaving soon. I felt a certain kind of comfort that night, being surrounded by family, and I started to feel like I didn't want to come back.

Two nights before going back home to America, I sat by the fireplace and cried. I would be losing everyone all over again, and what did I have to look forward to on the other side of my flight? Depression was sneaking up on me again. After returning home from my trip, my entire life spiraled out of control. Everything happened at once, and I had no idea where to start resolving my problems. I had just two weeks before school started, which I spent frantically rewriting my thesis. Although my boss had promised it to me, I never got my job back. My brother abruptly moved to another state, leaving me lonelier than ever before.

When life happens all at once in the negative way, you lose interest for living, and depression starts creeping up.

Day-in and day-out, I slept. I didn't eat—and, when I did, I made myself throw up. I felt useless. Helpless. I just wanted to go crawl into a hole and never come out. Every time I got up, *something* knocked me down; I was weakened by the struggles and the pain. It took a few months before I started to feel somewhat normal.

That's the thing with time: it heals all wounds, but the problem with that is, sometimes it takes a long time to get back to where we are ourselves again. In the meantime, some of that time is wasted on feeling sorry for ourselves.

CHAPTER FIVE

Solitude

In January of 2009, Amir moved to Rochester, Minnesota to live with his girlfriend. He couldn't *wait* to get out of Buffalo and away from all the family conflict. The fighting in our home became too much for the both of us to handle, but my brother was the one who decided to do something about it. Amir was smart enough to leave at the time that he did, and he never looked back.

Amir's move was the hardest on Mom. It was as if she became a different person, and her mental state was never the same. She cried constantly, became depressed and paranoid, blamed Dad and me for Amir's decision to leave, and even suggested that we forced him to leave. As the fights between my parents grew stronger, things at home became unbearable. They physically, mentally, and verbally abused one another. I didn't know how to fix anything, so I kept running—I had enough issues of my own and fixing my parents' marriage was not an issue I was able to tackle. One of the biggest problems in our family has always been our communication—or lack thereof. It seemed that my parents competed against each other for the title of Best Parent, forcing us to pick a side. Amir and I felt caught in the middle, and no choice was right.

I do not believe that children should be—or should be made to feel—responsible for fixing their parents' problems, but that scenario plays out more often than we'd like to admit. Those who stay together "for the sake of the children" hope to spare their kids the pressures of growing up in a "broken" family, but they are blind to the fact that their family is *already* broken. I felt the weight and pressure of family conflict growing up; I know that this supposed solution only prolongs a child's suffering.

Before my parents married, my mom was engaged to another man. The alleged story is that my dad showed up to my mom's house with the wedding party and took her home with him. Tata "stole" Mama from another man, and they eloped. When my mother's ex-fiancé came looking for her, she was already gone. He threw the ring she left behind into the creek at the base of my grandparents' house. My grandma looked for the ring for weeks, but she never ended up finding it.

After twenty-five years of marriage, my parents just stopped *liking* each other. As they so often do in these cases, rumors spread that tore down the barely-standing walls of their relationship. My parents lost touch with their friends, and Mama turned her back on her family. It already had been such a long time since she had spoken to them. Adults sometimes forget that they are not always right, and my mother was no exception. She believed that she was right about *everything*, that everyone else in the world was wrong or against her.

The stress of dealing with a person who refuses to believe something is wrong with them can be too much to handle. Sometimes I hated her for that. Her paranoia and extreme outbursts increased until the day I will never forget, the day my dad and I realized something was *seriously* wrong.

My mother had called the police. That morning, she woke me up to come downstairs and talk to the cops. My father, three officers, and two EMTs stood in the kitchen, all listening to mom explain how she *knew* that someone was watching her. I was scared, embarrassed, and just very confused. What was happening in my home? I could not, for the life of me, hold back my tears. I cried so hard and so loud as I begged her to stop.

An ambulance took Mom to the Erie County Medical Center and admitted her to the psychiatric center. She blamed that one on us, too. My mother had convinced herself that Tata and I were plotting against her, that everyone else was helping us out. *What is happening,* I asked myself, *and why in the Hell is it my fault?*

In my entire life, I had never seen anyone act the way my mother did that day. The doctors told us that Mom suffered from psychotic depression, a serious mood disorder that required hospitalization and medication. I was horrified to realize that I felt *relieved*—not just to have found an answer, but also because I did not have to be near her for a few days.

The house was peaceful: There was no fighting, screaming, or yelling. Dad went to work, I went to school, and everything was normal. I lived free of fear for a few days, and then Mom returned home. Her stay at the hospital proved essentially useless; everything returned to her kind of normal.

I avoided being at home as much as I could. I constantly stayed late at school, at a friend's house, or out partying. It was my escape from anything that had to do with my family. Dad grew tired of the blame game, so he went on a trip to visit family. The week I spent alone with my mother felt like a month. I hated every minute of it. I searched for a sign that I would be okay, but I was afraid for my life. I wanted to scream! I wanted someone to listen! I wanted someone to connect with me on an emotional level, but I was not going to receive that kind of attention from anyone in my family, so I did the best next thing: I spent most of my early twenties drinking away the pain and ignoring all of my responsibilities with people who had the worst possible influence on me.

Shoulder to Cry On

Throughout my college years, one of my favorite activities—and greatest escapes—was going out line dancing with my friends on Thursday nights. We'd dance all night, fall into bed at three in the morning, and wake up for work two hours later. We repeated this pattern once a week for almost ten years. One of these nights, I noticed a handsome guy sitting across the bar and asked my friends to introduce me. His name was Richard, or Dick for short. The night I met Dick altered my life in so many impossible-to-predict ways. Dick and I started dating in March of 2010. Our relationship filled the emotional void left by my troubled homelife: I finally had someone to talk to, someone to lean on, and someone to help me escape from my problems.

With Dick's presence in my life, I began to escape my misery. He helped me through my personal issues and encouraged me to grow as a person. It's no surprise that it took me a few short months to fall in love with him; I wanted nothing more than to spend time together, to be present and enjoying life. As it was my initial adult relationship, I experienced many of my "firsts" with Dick, and it was obvious to him—and to his family—that I was growing attached quickly.

His mother became an incredibly important person in my life. Every time I called, she picked up. Every time I arrived on her doorstep, she invited me in. It did not take long for this woman to become the mother figure that I was lacking. My own mother and I grew further apart, but Dick and his mom stood by me, regardless of my struggles at home.

As I fell in love with my new relationship, I also fell in love with life: there was beauty in every day and a smile on my face each morning. I couldn't help it—I was smitten. The summer we spent together that year couldn't have been better: we took care of each other, experienced new things, and laughed every day. I truly believed he was giving me the best he possibly could.

I loved driving up to visit Dick's family in the country. It was my getaway, my escape from everything. I spent many weekends there enjoying the peace and quiet—a rare luxury in my own home. We spent our time cooking, swimming, and fishing together. We played with the family's Chihuahuas, and I was happy to bond with my favorite dog, Molly.

The happier I became, the angrier my dad grew. My parents didn't approve of my new relationship, and I couldn't convince them otherwise. Dick was neither a Bosnian nor a Muslim, so my parents saw my choices as a disappointment to the family. I started to resent my parents because of this, and my relationship with them suffered dearly. They treated me as if I had committed an unforgiveable sin, and I couldn't understand how they could be mad at me for the crime of being *happy*.

I was crushed by their disappointment. What, exactly, had I done wrong? My sadness turned to animosity; I felt alone and heartbroken without the support of my parents. My family insisted that Dick and I would never have a future together, that we couldn't work out due to our differences. I didn't understand. If two people love and care for one another, why should differences of religion or culture matter?

In the end, my parents' wish came true. Dick made new friends, ones who introduced him to the finer things in life. He became fixated on acquiring better things, even using others to get his way. When we began dating, Dick had seemed happy with his life. He was ambitious about what he hoped to accomplish and made a genuine effort. Something happened along the way, and, as young people do, he changed into someone else. I no longer recognized the man with whom I had fallen in love.

New issues arose in our relationship. His different goals meant everything to him, and I became the least important person in his life. I wanted so desperately to resolve our problems, and I tried everything I knew: I gave him space, avoided fights, and ignored the things he did that hurt me, yet somehow the blame was always mine. He would tell me that I didn't—couldn't—know how relationships worked. He insisted that him sleeping with other women was, in fact, *good* for our relationship. He manipulated my feelings against me, knowing I'd let anything go because I loved him. I didn't know then that *love shouldn't hurt.*

Perhaps I loved Dick a bit too much, maybe even to the point of obsession. I thought that what we shared was special. I was desperate for a meaningful connection, and I thought I had found one with him. He used my longing and trust to manipulate me, to abuse me verbally. The signs had been clear from the beginning, but it was as if they were appearing before me for the first time. Our relationship was doomed from the start, but I chose to deny the truth. I cared for him more than I cared for myself, but to him I held no purpose. Ultimately, it taught me a valuable lesson.

Never rely on others for happiness; happiness comes from within us. Create your own, and you will create self-love.

I don't blame him for not loving me as much as I loved him. I was mostly angry at his lack of respect toward me—not just as his girlfriend, but as a person. I believe that, if he had loved himself as he was and the life we had at that time, maybe our relationship would have survived. Dick couldn't appreciate what he had; he always wanted more. While there is nothing wrong with wanting more in life, he chose to do it the wrong way. Our downfall was his lack of gratitude and the way he used the women around him for his own benefit. I hadn't quite learned what love *was*, but I now knew what love *wasn't*.

Broken

On Christmas Eve of 2001, it was hard for me to feel the holiday spirit that had uplifted me in my youth. Tata was frustrated with Mom and left us that morning; I was forced to deal with her demons alone. I tried to hold back my tears as I drove to work, carrying on with my day as best I could.

Later that day, I sat on the floor of my room, surrounded by Christmas gifts, trying to decide whether I should spend the holidays alone or with the one person I loved more than anything, but who in fact, did not love me back. I felt trapped in a never-ending nightmare, but I still hoped to escape the darkness. The pain became numbness. I couldn't even cry anymore.

Dick's parents insisted that I spend Christmas Eve with them at his cousin's house. He was so close but so far away—I was dying on the inside and yet afraid to reach out to him. I was a stranger now; I no longer belonged. Uncomfortable and afraid, I waited in a daze, hoping he would make a move. At the end of the night, he sat next to me, put his arm around me, and pretended that everything was okay for the rest of the evening. I knew he would avoid the problems that were tearing us apart, that this silent exchange would be the closest we would come to communication.

On Christmas morning, I made my way up to his house. The once-familiar drive was torture. One million thoughts flew through my head; I played out one thousand conversations between us and examined every detail one hundred times. I still had a knot in my stomach, an instinct that something was wrong, and I realized, at that moment, that there was no coming back from this. I was never going to win this fight.

Lying in his arms that night, I knew—*just knew*— that it would be the last time. He got up and left, exactly as he always did, but everything was already different. I argued with myself that he just needed more time, that the new year would set things right. I couldn't have been more wrong.

I celebrated New Year's Eve with Dick's parents.

We had planned to meet at the casino. I waited for him for hours, but he never showed up. He had spent the night with someone else. I felt humiliated, rejected, and completely broken. By this point, he had torn me apart. I truly believed him when he told me that I would be nothing without him, that I had nothing to offer him, that I knew nothing about relationships, and that no one would want me because I was damaged. I was fully convinced that I was the problem.

Although we were no longer together, he made it nearly impossible to forget our past. When I did see him, he was there but never present. I thought we were trying to make things work, but it became apparent that only I was trying; he was simply getting what he wanted, even at my expense. I gave Dick every ounce of love that I had within me, but he wasn't strong enough to carry that weight. He was just a boy controlling a grown man's body, and I kept waiting for him to grow up.

When I realized my efforts were wasted, I went on, slowly, with my life—but, every now and again, I'd be reminded of him, of *us*, and the cycle of heartbreak would begin all over again. It took me two-and-a-half years to get over Dick and fall out of love with him completely.

I loved him entirely, but I will always love him more for breaking my heart and setting me free. I was forced to learn to stand up for myself, to fight against the negativity that tore my life apart for three years. I learned to love myself, growing stronger despite the ways I had been conditioned to tear myself down. On the day I accepted that I no longer needed—or even wanted—him in my life, I felt relieved. Lighter. My heart pieced itself together, and I began to live again.

The three most important men in my life were gone. I understood Amir's decision to leave, and now he was building a new life with his wife and their baby on the way. Even though we lived states apart, Amir and I tried to keep in touch as much as possible. We never wanted to lose our close bond. When my brother became a father, it was so special for all of us. I couldn't wait to meet my baby niece and hold her in my arms.

Despite the joy of our new addition to the family, I couldn't accept the fact that my dad had left, and my brother's gain highlighted my loss. By now, I no longer feared being alone, but resentment consumed me. I

111

only grew angrier the worse Mama got. With no guidance from my family, I had to rely on my friends—and, often, myself—for the sake of my health and sanity.

About four months after my dad left, Mama and I traveled to Minnesota to meet Amir's baby girl. I was reunited with my brother and met my beautiful niece. For a moment, it seemed enough to me.

In light of everything good, something bad always follows.

Tata showed up unexpectedly at Amir's home. It was the first time Mama and I had seen or spoken to him since the day he decided to leave us. Everyone put on a brave face, trying our hardest not to ruin the thus-far decent trip. It wasn't enough, though. I couldn't even look at my father, because seeing him just reminded me of how hurt he had left me. No one knew the battles I fought; no one in my family thought to ask about the ugly truths I locked up away in my mind. I realized then that I couldn't really know what the rest of them were dealing with either.

CHAPTER SIX

Unstable

The universe was plotting against me, I figured. I shielded myself away from every breathing soul. I had been dealt some pretty hard punches, and I had no idea how to hit back. I battled with the balance of life as though I walked on an unstable wire being pulled toward one side. Unstable wires tend to bend, and life challenged me to figure out how to straighten the line back to its original position. Falling from the wire, I realized the source of its pull: my mother. Every day felt like a living Hell: like nails on a chalkboard that never stopped, day-in and day-out. I would wake up every morning to her yelling and go to bed every night to the same sound.

Being around her felt like being in limbo with no

113

chance of moving forward. As much as I tried, I couldn't figure out how to help her—and part of me wondered if perhaps she didn't deserve help either, because of the way she treated me.

I didn't understand. I kept asking, "Why me?" repeatedly. Words alone cannot describe the strength necessary for living alongside someone battling severe mental illness. It is something that cannot be known until it is experienced, and it is not an experience I would wish upon anyone. Distress consumed me completely. I lived each day with stress and fear from which there was no escape. So many times, I wished that I could just go to sleep and never wake up. Looking back, I ask myself this: if I felt such despair dealing with my mother, *how did she feel dealing with her own mind?*

The idea of a peaceful mind and a soul at ease became important but unimaginable to me, and I just couldn't catch a break. My daily anxiety consisted of the uncertainty of what might happen to her—or what she would do to me—if one of the episodes became too much for her to handle. I felt an enormous weight on my shoulders: I was the daughter of an ill mother,

LIFE LOVES ME, LIFE LOVES ME NOT

someone who was supposed to be the closest person to me but was the furthest away. I learned quickly that certain things were better off left unsaid, even if it hurt me to hold back. I suppressed my feelings out of concern; the last thing I wanted was to be the trigger of her episodes.

I became afraid for a different reason too. I worried that, if I didn't do something about it soon, one day it could be *me*. More than anything, I feared becoming a monster, which is exactly what she seemed like to me during that time. I let her words slip past me; I forgave her every day, even if I couldn't stand it. My role was to keep the peace between us, but I didn't believe I was strong enough to deal with such a delicate situation. I knew, in one sense, that none of it was my fault, but I still blamed myself. On some days I even wished I wasn't alive. I resented that I had not worked harder, that I always had to rely on my parents. I wished I had the audacity to leave like Amir did, and I imagined how differently things would have turned out if I had.

That May, I took a much-needed break by escaping to Florida to visit my friend Amra. I needed something else in my life besides the constant fear and pain. I needed to recharge, and what better way could there be than spending my birthday at Disney World and passing time at the beach? For a moment, all my problems disappeared, just as they always did when I had a chance to explore a new corner of the world.

Having a loved one suffer through paranoia, hallucinations, and pain was a nightmare for me; I can't even imagine what it felt like for her. I lived every day hoping for the best but always preparing for the worst. For her to be able to overcome this disease, she would need professional guidance—but how do you convince a crazy person that they are crazy? My mother turned against me every single day, and I let her. I tried so hard to give up on the possibility of her getting better and helping her—but, as much as she hurt me every day, part of me just couldn't turn my back on her.

It was a perfect storm: I had grown accustomed to emotional and verbal abuse in my past relationship— though no one should have to get used to something like that—so I knew how to play the same role for my mother. With my self-worth deteriorated, I knew what to expect and how to manage it. I strove to be a decent person—I've always gotten along with everyone—but, I couldn't find the balance between being accommodating and being put down, and I just couldn't let her control me anymore.

My mother was impossible to read. I never knew what she needed exactly, and she made loving her unbearable. She considered me her worst enemy. Although there was no one she trusted—not family, not friends—I was still the only person she had. I tiptoed around her and avoided any interaction, always at the ready for the next fight. That was my only defense mechanism: not saying anything at all and being prepared.

I often wonder when her illness started developing. Did it begin when she was just a child, waiting all this time for a chance to take hold? Was it when she was a teenager, growing into her new mind and body? Did it happen during the war, brought on by all the struggles she faced and the weight she carried as a daughter, wife, and mother? Her perspective was her reality; there was no other way around it. In her eyes, only her truth became true, and everything around her became a lie. I spent little time at home. I worked as much as I could because I feared going home and sleeping in my own bed.

Her condition deteriorated after Amir's accident. I no longer had the strength to convince her of the damage she caused herself—and me. I began to understand that, until she accepted the fact that she had a real problem, we could make no progress. I was helpless to change her feelings. I couldn't fight her demons for her, and nothing would change that.

The Storm

On Sunday, June 8th of 2014, my world came crashing down once again. I woke up looking forward to a fun day I had planned with friends, but I couldn't have anticipated what life itself planned for me. I received a message from my cousin, Ena. Why was Ena, who lived in Des Moines, Iowa, messaging me?

Hi, Mirela. Amir was in a car accident. He is in a critical condition. Please call your dad. We don't know if he is going to make it.

Without hesitation, I jumped out of bed and called my father. A few years had passed since we last spoke, but I could hear the heartbreak in his voice. Amir wasn't doing well; he had spent the night in the emergency room on life support and was waiting to go into surgery. Distraught and in complete shock, I tried to wrap my head around this dreadful news. I rushed downstairs, frantic and sobbing, to tell my mom what had happened. I gasped for air as if I was drowning and fought to get the words out through my tears.

We heard a knock on the door. A police officer stood on our front porch. It had been so long since Mom and I had kept in touch with my father that he did not have any means of contacting us, so he asked the local police to deliver the news. As soon as the police officer saw me, he realized that I already knew what he had come to tell me. Endless questions flashed through my mind:

> *What do I do?*
> *Where do I begin?*
> *How do I handle this?*

And, most importantly, *how in the world do I convince my mother that this truly happened?* Everything was a conspiracy to my mother; I knew right away that she wouldn't believe any of it. Of course, she remained in denial. I messaged back and forth with my cousin, trying to figure out how to get there. I wanted to be by my brother's side to help him recover—or to be there in case he didn't make it through.

The pressure I felt on my chest kept digging deeper into my body. I knew I needed to be with my brother, but I also needed to explain to Mom what happened, to convince her it was real. Her mistrust, delusions, and detachment from reality complicated everything. She became completely disinterested in listening to anything I needed to say, so I didn't say anything at all. I decided to take care of what I could on my own. She didn't want to be a part of it, so I didn't make her.

In the days following the accident, I scrambled to come up with the funds for a plane ticket. My aunt offered to pay for my travel expenses, but I hated the idea of asking for help, especially when it came to money. I felt I had no choice but to accept the offer. Emotionally exhausted, I met my friends for dinner in the hopes of shutting off my overtired brain for a little while. Heather, one of my good friends, told me not to worry about the money for the plane ticket: she and a few others were chipping in to buy one for me so that I could be with family. I couldn't believe that despite everything happening in this chaotic time, the amazing people I call my friends genuinely wanted to help. *I wish everyone has the kind of friends that I do, because they are the best in the world.*

On June 7th, 2014, I flew out to Des Moines. At this point, it had been about three years since I had last seen my dad, and I was nervous to finally see him face-to-face. Once I landed and made my way down to the baggage claim, I saw my father and Ena waiting for me in the distance. It felt like it took forever to reach them; my anxiety began acting up as I slowly approached. In front of me stood a middle-aged man. He looked older and more worn down than the last time I saw him; his hair was grayer, but it shined in the fluorescent light like pure silver. His skin held the same tone as mine, yet his was dotted with more freckles and lines that defined his age. He hugged me so hard that I couldn't breathe. It felt like a good time to forgive him for leaving.

Tata and I shared a pleasant conversation back at the apartment where he lived with Amir. He apologized for leaving me behind—and for not realizing how sick Mama had become. I was cautious at first, but soon I opened up to him, explaining everything that I had been through since he left. He listened and apologized repeatedly. When it was time to unpack, I settled in Amir's room, where I would be staying for the length of the trip. I took in my surroundings and thought about my brother. He was always so organized; every little thing had its own place, and everything in there seemed so sad without him.

We headed over to my aunt and uncle's house. I hadn't seen them in eight years or so. My cousin was all grown up; it was so hard to believe! I remembered Ena as a tomboy, always playing with Amir, and now she had become this beautiful young woman. We picked up right where we left off—it didn't feel as though we hadn't spoken in so long, but more as though we had never stopped. It was time to drive to the hospital to see Amir. His body rested there on the bed, lifeless, hooked up to so many different machines to help him breathe. The image immediately seared itself into my memory.

Amir's brain was swollen from the massive hit he took to his head in the car accident. The doctors performed a surgery that they called a *decompressive craniectomy*, which meant they'd remove part of his skull to allow room for the brain to swell. The entire right side of his head was swollen, and he had an enormous scar from his ear to the right side of his forehead. It was sewn up with what must have been a hundred stitches. I stood there and watched Dad talk to him, saying, *"Please wake up!"* My eyes filled with tears, and my heart hurt so bad. What came next was harder: the nurse told us he didn't look good at all, that if the swelling didn't go down, he wouldn't make it. She asked me to talk to my family about pulling the plug.

Everything just seemed so *unreal*. I wished, uselessly, to wake up from this horrible nightmare, and that's exactly what it was: a nightmare, but very real. I had hoped Amir would wake up while I was there, but we didn't have such luck.

The rest of the family tried to make the best of our reunion, despite the circumstances. I spent time exploring the city with Ena. We went to eat at *Apare,* one of Amir's favorite Japanese restaurants. I was surprised and delighted to find that Des Moines had such a large Bosnian community—it almost felt like I was back home in Bosnia. Everywhere we went, we encountered the Bosnian language, Bosnian restaurants, and Bosnian grocery stores. The familiarity, however unexpected, was comforting.

Even though Mom didn't believe that Amir had been in an accident, she called me repeatedly—almost every five minutes—to let me know that I had disappointed her for "choosing" my father's side, that I would regret it for the rest of my life. Her only son was in the hospital, fighting for his life, and she told me that she hoped I was dead.

I tried not to take her words to heart. She didn't understand; her illness wouldn't let her understand. It had taken over. Her reality consisted of fear, and she didn't see what the rest of us did. But still, what she said dug at my emotional wounds. I felt guilty for being with family, like I was unable to appreciate the progress my father and I had made or the bond I had rekindled with my cousin. I had hoped to find some peace throughout this ordeal, but now I felt forced to constantly defend myself.

It was time for me to leave, and Amir still wasn't waking up. I was terrified of leaving him behind, but I knew he had some exceptionally strong and kind people by his side. Upon returning home, I sat down with Mama: I wanted to tell her everything, to show her pictures of Amir in the hospital bed, clinging to life. She believed only that I told her lies, so I made my final decision to keep her in the dark. I reminded her what had happened, from time to time, when she asked me why he wouldn't answer her calls, but I was not able to convince her of anything.

My friends rallied together to create a great support system for me during this time, especially Lisa, whom I affectionately call *Booboo*. I couldn't have asked for a better person to help me keep my head up high amid all the pain and sadness. I spent many nights on her couch, crying myself to sleep when I feared being at home. I spent just as many lying awake, trying to come up with a plan for my future that was peaceful—and with a little less pain.

CHAPTER SEVEN

Revelation

I was a year away from my thirtieth birthday, and I was feeling like an absolute failure. I judged myself more than anyone else had ever judged me in my entire life. I was ashamed that I wasn't proud of my place in life; I didn't think others would be proud of me—or even approve. I felt unsuccessful because I wasn't using my college degree and worked a job that gave me anxiety, a job that I didn't really consider a career. I had all the friends I could ask for, but I still felt like the loneliest person in the world. Sometimes I still do.

I couldn't figure out how to move forward. I was tired of not having anything to show for myself. I needed to make some major changes in my life before I wasted my precious years just living to survive. I wanted to experience life in a different light and learn new things.

I needed to seek my own self-fulfillment before I regretted not doing enough in my life. Everyone is in this world to make some kind of difference—I just want to make a big one.

I decided to write a letter to my future self, to the person I so badly wanted to become. I made a list of things I wanted to achieve and started crossing them off, one-by-one. As I worked through my list, I began to feel more accountable and eager to achieve better things for myself. I needed to make my own life a priority and take care of myself in every sense. In my years of unhappiness, I missed out on so much of what life had to offer. For the first time, however, I *looked forward* to making a change. I got my first tattoo and signed up for an online class to brush up on my interior design skills. I took up Spanish lessons again and planned a vacation to Mexico with my friend Marie. For months, I practiced Spanish so I would be able to use it on my vacation. I watched movies, binged telenovelas, and listened to Latin music. Taking on a more positive attitude provided me with the ambition and motivation to work for the things I truly wanted.

I was eager to visit my personal idea of paradise and take much-needed time off from reality. Our Mexican adventure took us to the beautiful town of Playa Del Carmen for a six-day, all-inclusive vacation. That day, the airport was just as magical as the one in Italy had been all those years ago. The people-watching, the planes landing and taking off, the amazing feeling of adventure that stirred the excitement within me, and the amazing view of the world you get from thousands of miles off the ground: everything was as I remembered. We enjoyed our flight—and some mimosas. As our plane descended in Cancun, the view of the ocean was absolutely breathtaking.

After landing and passing through Customs, we headed to the baggage claim. We hailed a taxi and enjoyed mild air conditioning on our way to the resort. I was stunned, emotional, and in awe of the many beautiful things I glimpsed through the window—and of the tragic images I saw, as well. On one side of the highway stood grand and beautiful resorts; on the other side, stray dogs ran amongst disheveled huts built from wooden panels, palm trees, and plastic bags. It reminded me of the refugee camps where I spent my childhood.

We approached the gated community of the Playcar, and everything looked like a picture: strikingly beautiful condos and resorts stood cookie-cutter, one next to the other. Locals and visitors strolled down the street, rode their bikes, zoomed past on scooters, or jogged through the beautiful avenues. I fell in love with the condos down there, each one more beautiful than the other, only to dream of one day maybe owning one. We arrived at a beautiful resort that was everything we expected—and even more. I felt fortunate to be able to take this trip and experience another piece of the world, one I never dreamed I would experience. Our room overlooked the lovely garden filled with wildlife, the amazing sounds of nature, and the waterfall centerpiece. Once we settled in, we took a stroll down to the beach.

You know how, when you see a beautiful picture of a white-sand beach and a mesmerizing sunset with colors so vibrant, you take a little trip in your own head? It awakens this joy inside of you, and you think to yourself, "I wish I could be there *right now*." I was experiencing that fantasy, one that I never thought would happen in my wildest dreams, *but it was there in reality*. I was standing with my feet deep in the warm sand, gazing out at the beautiful Caribbean as the sun set. The ocean waves were slowly crashing into the edge of the shore, and I was filled with a calm excitement. My soul felt at peace: stress-free, like I was, at last, able to breathe. I felt like I *belonged* on that beach.

I experienced a flashback of my entire life and my journey so far in this world up to that exact moment. I felt such gratitude for my life. I appreciated everything I had.

Mexican cuisine has always been one of my favorites. I lived for tacos and margaritas and enjoyed many aspects of Mexican culture. I loved reading about the history of the country and learning about its culture and traditions. To have the chance to experience all these wonderful things felt unreal. Taking a moment to talk to the locals and learn about their way of life made me feel extremely thankful for all the things I had: my family and friends, my job, a car to take me places, the roof over my head, and the food on my table. I had to work a fraction of how much my new friends needed to work to earn a week's worth of pay. It put many things into perspective, and I truly realize that not everyone is as lucky as I have been. This was more than a vacation: it was a learning experience that taught me value of life.

Our adventure in paradise included many entertaining excursions. We took a bus one morning to a *hacienda* for a Mexican-style horseback ride, in the Mayan Riviera. The tour guide took us through the jungle along a path that showcased the beautiful vegetation of our tropical surroundings. There was wildlife everywhere, accompanied by the comforting sounds of nature. We tried natural gum made from Zapote and Chicozpote trees, which grow in the tropical jungles of the Yucatan Peninsula in Mexico, and we learned that this product would biodegrade within two weeks, unlike from the usual gum we chew. We experienced a view of *cenote*s, or sinkholes, up close, and gazed into its depth of one hundred feet or more down into the ground. The water was crystal clear, and you could see the rocks at its jagged bottom.

We rode our horses back to the ranch and got a chance to cool off in a *cenote* that was eight feet deep. The water was cold, but the swim itself was refreshing in the eighty-five-degree weather. We enjoyed snacks and ice-cold beverages. We explored the ranch, taking in its beauty and snapping some pictures of the donkeys, horses, monkeys, and peacocks. I felt like I was living one of the vibrant scenes of the telenovelas I adored.

The next day, our adventure took us to Punta Tanachate in Bahi Petompian Puerto Morales for a snorkeling session. We arrived at this awesome beach club surrounded by the tallest palm trees, tiki bars, and picnic tables. We were accompanied by other tourists on a thirty-four-foot boat, that took us out to the Caribbean's deep water, for our first session of snorkeling. We swam over the beautiful coral and came very close to a turtle and a stingray.

Our guides treated us to an authentic Mexican meal of grilled chicken, Mexican rice and beans, homemade chips and salsa, and some well-deserved cold drinks. After the meal, we relaxed under the thatched umbrellas and took naps in rainbow-colored hammocks, before going back in the water for the rest of our snorkeling session. I loved being surrounded by nothing except water, the calming noises of the ocean, and a cool breeze. This made for one of our most perfect days in paradise. I grew more aware of how much good Mother Nature does for our soul and how much love she feeds us—of how we need to take care of her in return.

I fell deeply in love with this little town, and I felt extremely thankful to have the opportunity to experience it. Our final exploration, my absolute favorite, was also the most educational: visiting the sacred ground and the ancient temples of Chichen Itza. After arriving to the beautiful Maylands Resort, we got a chance to walk around and take some pictures before the tour started. This resort was breathtaking. Everything—from the high ceilings and decorative chandeliers to the beautiful antique furniture that represented the tastefully rich Latin décor, to the colorful tiles with mesmerizing prints—made me feel like I could stay there forever and be perfectly content. The porch was surrounded with tall bamboo, along with other variety of plants and trees. The fountains' soothing sound of falling water, straw huts far and wide, and beautiful green grass made this resort seem like it was built on an entirely different planet.

As we began the tour through the ancient village of the Mayan and the Toltec people that occupied the city nearly three thousand years before, I was overtaken by how it felt to be part of something so tremendous and experience its beauty. The architectural detail on every stone wall and the history of each structure was beyond belief; it felt like quite a treasure to be given this information. It is something you can't know until you experience it. Standing in front of the Great Kulkan Pyramid made me realize, once again, how fortunate I was to see it with my own eyes.

It also taught me how big our entire world is—we can't understand that until we experience something grand, something that makes us appreciate all the pieces of our world. We all, individually, are just one person, but what surrounds us is bigger than all of us together.

The entire trip simply left me in awe, and I grew curious for what the rest of the world had to offer. This, by far, was one of my favorite things I got to experience that year. In my travels, I connected with strangers and made new friends. If it weren't for that trip, I would have never met an amazing couple from Chicago who are now my friends, Jenn and Donny. Now, three years later, we will be all returning to paradise for Jenn and Donny's beach wedding. I am constantly reminded of what I learned in Mexico, as I keep in touch with—and visit—the people with whom I experienced that magical vacation. If we are lucky enough to meet people from all walks of life and exchange stories, everyone makes a mark on one another. We learn from each other, and if everyone is as fortunate as I am, you get to make friends for life. I concluded my trip to Mexico by making a lifelong promise to myself: to always take time for *me* and to feed my soul with everything the world has to offer.

Arriving home from my adventure had left me in a serious post-travel depression; I was anxious with the realization that I was not ready to return to the unsatisfying reality of everyday life. My hunger for travel grew more intense, and I finally felt in-touch with my desires. I felt like, in my mind, I had painted a picture of what life could—and should—be like.

Although I couldn't articulate it at the time, I was overwhelmed with a sense of *knowing* what I wanted to live for: experiences, both big and small; adventures, both long and short; and challenges, both hard and easy.

No matter how challenging my life had been before, a little bit of heaven pushed me; it motivated me to accomplish the things that are necessary so I can enjoy the things that I desire.

Time felt like one of my worst enemies. Life kept moving onward, slipping away from me—and, every time I grew close to taking a step forward, the force of the universe held me back. I wanted, *so badly*, to arrive at the place where things are okay—as though it might be a physical location I could find, and not a state of mind. I wanted my world to be a bit better organized. I didn't expect perfection, not by any means, but I wanted to worry a little less and be happy a little more often.

No one was left to rescue me, but I didn't expect anyone to anyway. I don't think anyone has ever figured it all out at once. I'm no exception, and I was starting to find myself perfectly okay with that. I tried to maintain positivity, despite what life had thrown at me. Back in my post-vacation reality, I was working two jobs just to pay the bills, coping with a mentally ill parent, and still trying to make something of myself. How could I blame myself for sometimes feeling weak and uncertain? It's okay to take time to feel sad, to mourn, to move through your self-pity. There is nothing wrong with having a good cry: it's a healthy part of growing as a human being. Accept the cards you have been dealt, and find a way to move past it. Trust me: as soon as you do, your entire world changes.

I knew things would have to be different in order to be better: that I'd have to level beyond what I thought I could handle and step out of the comfortable bubble in which I had confined myself. I had to take a chance on every opportunity; it was the only way I'd learn what I liked about myself. I had fallen victim to the pressure of expectations, the thought that I had to, in some way, accomplish all my goals by a certain age. I couldn't have been more wrong.

Monster Within

It had taken me nearly seven years to convince my mother to seek help for her illness, and it had taken me just as long to realize that all the signs had been there my entire life—that I had been, indeed, growing up in a mentally ill household. Both of my parents have been prone to outbursts and extreme highs and lows. As the oldest child, I had been witnessing their fights since I could remember. I experienced years and *years* of their back-and-forth, pointlessly arguing who was right and who was wrong. I became accustomed to unpredictability, but I never questioned it. I simply hoped for a "good" day, pretending that it was more than enough for me. Bad days were worse than you could imagine—and they clouded over even the good days, because I always felt that the next episode was right around the corner.

Because we were always on the verge of the next

disaster, I avoided going anywhere with my mother. This, in turn, only caused her to think that I was against her, that I had negative intentions—and I just didn't want to deal with it. She found it difficult to explain what she was going through: this was her reality, and whatever hallucinations she was experiencing were very real to her. She grew more frustrated at the fact that no one else was able to see what she was seeing. Her journey into madness became so much worse. Frustrated by her inability to share her world, she lashed out at me, because I was the only person in her life at this point.

She withdrew, isolating herself from everything and everyone; she was deranged and hysterical, confused and depressed. I was only capable of being there, distanced far enough to protect myself from harm while watching to ensure she did not harm herself. She always thought I was hiding something and pried for any information. I was embarrassed that this was who my mother had become, that I was related to this *insane* person—but I also felt guilty for having these terrible thoughts. My mother and I lived under the same roof, but we shared no closeness. Unstable and disoriented, Mom was admitted, once more, to the psychiatric hospital and behavioral unit of the Erie County Medical Center of Buffalo, New York.

That September of 2016, I was overcome with both concern and peace-of-mind. At first, I was happy, but then I would break down. Then I was okay, but then I was not. After a few days, I was able to calm down and rearrange the thoughts in my head. The first day that I visited her was almost unbearable. As soon as my mother saw me, she began to blame me. It was my fault that she was there, it was my fault that she wasn't allowed to go home, and I was conspiring against her with the doctors. She couldn't help herself. After talking to the nurses and the social worker, I felt relieved to learn that she wasn't going anywhere for a while. I thought to myself, *I'm safe from her, if only for a few days.*

The doctors diagnosed her with severe depression, psychosis, and schizophrenia. They also told me that her paranoia will never go away, that she will have to live with it for the rest of her life. As difficult as that was for me to hear, it was even harder for her. Mom said she felt like she was in jail; she called me at least thirty times and left just as many voicemails. I didn't listen to them they always contained the same message:

"Get me out of here!"
"I don't belong here!"
"I will never forgive you for this!"
"This is all your fault!"

She made me feel awful about wanting to help her; she was only preoccupied with what was in her head. I couldn't convince her that, in the long run, this would be so much better for her—for the both of us.

It took about a week of in-patient treatment for my mother to calm down. She wasn't thrilled about her confinement, but she managed the best she could, especially considering that she was surrounded by patients with even more severe disorders than hers. I visited her every other day, bringing her meals and snacks from the outside and some warmer clothing. I was happy to learn from the nurses that her attitude had changed drastically in that week. She began to laugh and smile when I came to visit—she even drew me a picture. I felt as though she was starting over, like a child learning to walk and speak. She was prescribed several medications, and they seemed to help.

It takes a lot for a person to comprehend that you may need to turn to medication for help in order to live a somewhat normal life.

Of course, she had neither healthcare nor the means to pay for this medication. Medical bills just kept piling up, but I kept telling myself, "We will figure it out; *we have to*—things can't be this hard forever." With medication, her manic outbursts and paranoia began to fall under control, although her depression lingered. As my mother began healing, I was forced to reevaluate our relationship. The past ten years had strained us; her new reality was difficult for me to process. Over the years, we had thrown vulgar insults at each other, and the scars, while faded, remained. She spent many years losing the battle to her mental demons, and I just wasn't built to handle it the right way. She blamed me, but I blamed her back. She yelled; I yelled back. On and on and on.

Everything is much calmer now—yet, after years of negativity, it's still a challenge to break down the barriers. To open to the possibility of caring is to open to the possibility of getting hurt—what if she were to stop taking her medication? We'd be back to where we were before, and that terrifies me. I kept the wall halfway up. It's not just for her, though; I kept that partial wall standing for anyone who came into my life after years of uncertainty and heartbreak.

Once my mother was released from the hospital, reality hit, and we needed to figure out how to deal with it. She had been laid off from work for a few months prior to her hospital visit, but, in her altered state, she didn't realize the severity of the problems that had accumulated over the years. Her lack of steady employment meant she was living off a second mortgage with minimal income, and the bills were piling up—that's bound to get a person in trouble.

My family has always had more bad luck than good when it came to financial security, but that little bit of good luck always proved to me that things, in some way or another, were going to work themselves out for the better.

You can't just have good or bad; you must have both. That's the only way. It taught me how to survive and how to become stronger when your world crashes down. You need both to have balance in life.

CHAPTER EIGHT

Light in the Dark

Everything changed quickly after Mom got out of the hospital. Things were peaceful, and it felt strange. For so long, I had to deal with *discomposure*—long enough to get used to it. This new behavior? Well, I didn't quite know how to process it. The peace and quiet were amazing! There was no fighting, there wasn't any yelling, and things were getting better. Most shockingly of all, Mom finally requested that we visit Amir at his rehabilitation facility! I had no idea how to handle this turn of events, so I called my father for help. Although my parents hadn't spoken with one another in over six years, he agreed. I couldn't imagine how this new development would play out, but I felt instinctively nervous of the outcome.

For all that had happened over the years, this change felt somehow more enormous. Mom bought a ticket to Des Moines, planning to stay with Dad for four days. I had to remind him to stay calm: even though my mother was in a significantly better mental state, she still had no idea what was waiting for her. This would be her first-time seeing Amir in almost four years. The rest of us had spent that time processing our heartbreak over the extent of his injuries; Mom would be confronting it all for the first time.

Mama was, just then, feeling raw pain. As a mother, processing the immense tragedy of her child's accident must have been her hardest challenge yet. She needed everything to be explained to her as if the wounds were fresh: what had happened, how it had happened, and if Amir would ever be the same again. After four years of him living in a rehab center, disabled with little to no improvement, it was easy for all of us to feel discouraged. It was testing for us to keep hope of things ever getting better.

I challenged myself to view Amir's recovery from a different perspective. I thought, *never say never*, because no one can know how life will play itself out.

To this day, despite years without major improvement, I still believe that my brother will get his miracle one day, that he will get up out of that damn wheelchair and walk again. I understand how difficult and frustrating it is for a person to recover from a traumatic brain injury, but I refuse to believe that he has run out of options, that this is the pattern of the rest of his life. My brother *needs* to get better. He has a daughter that hardly knows him, and he is missing what should have been the most precious moments of his life. He knows he has her to fight for, though: the saddest moments are when he asks for her, crying, "Where is my daughter?" through his tears. There is nothing we can do. He has lost one of the biggest parts of him: his child.

After Mom returned home, she became much more worried. She had gotten a temp job, but it wasn't what she wanted. She wanted something better, something safer, something with benefits and medical insurance. Who could blame her? Isn't that what we all want? We all strive for a safe job that makes good enough money to pay our bills and lets us save for retirement; we don't want to worry about our basic needs. Everyone, unfortunately, can agree that finding such a position is a quite difficult, and settling for *good enough* is heartbreaking.

After much consideration, Mom made the decision to sell our house and move to Des Moines, Iowa. She was ready to be closer to Amir. After four months, the house sold; it was another major change that left me feeling unprepared.

Change is good, change is healthy, and change forces us to make decisions that we would not normally make: the decisions we want to make but are generally afraid to dive into.

I had a major decision to make. Would I relocate with my mom to a place that held no interest for me, or would I stay in Buffalo without my family? I chose to stay in Buffalo. I was not ready to leave, and I felt, instinctively, that my story there hadn't finished yet. As it turned out, there was more there for me than I could have anticipated.

In March of 2017, I finally moved out of my mother's house and moved in with my friend, Jacquie. The apartment was so different, so much smaller than the house—but it was an exciting new chapter in my life that needed to be written. As I settled in, certain events in my life began to unfold that left me excited about the direction in which I was headed. I, more than anything, fell in love with finding positivity in everything, even in the worst of circumstances.

I finally started feeling like I was getting things done, that my life was moving in the right direction. I was learning things about myself that I had never known before. I had been skeptical of people who said that their thirties were their best years, but soon I understood more than ever. It had never been about how much it sucks getting older or the amazing material things you have acquired; it was all about your new perspective. That's not to say you stop caring altogether; that's not it: you simply stop caring about the stupid bullshit, about the things in life you can't change. You start concentrating on things that matter, things that will provide you with self-fulfillment in the long run.

Ask yourself, "Is this, in any way, going to affect me in five years?" If not, then let it go.

Ever since I was a little girl, fawning over both telenovelas and blockbuster hits, I had dreamt of the glamor and artistry of acting. I loved performing in my childhood dance troupe and in high school musicals, but I didn't begin to consider the possibility more seriously until my junior year. I asked my drama teacher for advice, only to be told that such a dream was too hard to accomplish, and that I would not be good at it. Despite this unfriendly advice, the kind no ambitious child should have to hear, I never stopped dreaming. In college, I renewed my attempts. I went to auditions and even tried some modeling, but my goals always felt way out of my reach. Eventually, I began to feel that I was growing too old, that I would never make it in the entertainment industry, that my dream of becoming an actor would never become a reality. It wasn't until five years later that another opportunity fell into my lap. I told myself, *it's now or never.*

In the thirteen years or so since my high school days, I have transitioned the memory of my teacher, telling me that I would never be good enough into a motivational tool for my future. I know I'll have my share of rejections: *no, you're not good enough, you don't have the right look*, or *we think we are going with someone else*. I realize that, if you have that burning passion within you and are committed to the hard work that your dreams require, you just might make it. This new passion had given me the enthusiasm to take new risks and put myself out there.

Acceptance

Every day, I was working harder on making my dreams come true, and I was loving every second of it. My parents had become extremely supportive. They were willing to back me with anything I needed to make my dreams a reality, despite all that we had been through. I realized that this was precisely the right time for me to begin this journey. I started taking an acting class, and it brought so much joy to my life. I learned valuable lessons and met wonderful people: teachers and fellow classmates who have become my friends.

The first time I ever set a foot on a set, I was working as a background actor for my friend, Emir Skalonja. The universe really does work in extremely mysterious ways, and, for my first opportunity to come from someone who just happened to be from Bosnia as well? It was quite the sign.

When it's the right time, the universe will let you know. If something is supposed to happen, it will find you—just not always when you want it.

I am so thankful for that first opportunity, because it opened a door towards my dream. I am nowhere close to where I want to be, but I am working harder than ever before to get there. There are so many new things I want to experience, explore, and learn. My list is growing longer, and I am looking forward to my new adventures.

Life is not picture-perfect, not by any means. No matter how hard we try, we must experience both good and bad. I feel fortunate enough to have had the life I've lived. Have I loved every aspect of my experience so far? Absolutely not. I may often wish I could go back and do things differently, but that is not an option. The one and only option I *do* have is to use my past as a learning tool for my future.

I am a thirty-two-year-old woman with so much more life in front of me. I would like to do more every day, to accomplish things that drive me to be smarter and more committed. I have repeated the same mistakes so many times that I have lost count—and you'd think that anyone would learn the first time, or that we'd learn from the advice our parents and friends give us, but it doesn't matter. In the end, we'll keep making our mistakes until we take off our blinders and realize, *"Well, shit, this is not going to work. Maybe it's actually time I try it a different way."*

If you had asked me all those years ago, as a little girl in Bosnia, what my adult life would be like, I never would have anticipated this. As time progresses, you may not understand why things are happening the way they are, but, years later, it will hit you like a ton of bricks. *If it weren't for* that, *I wouldn't be in* this *situation*, you'll realize, for times both good and bad. Isn't it funny how everything in life comes full circle? I think it's either to bite you on the ass or pat you on the back.

To this day I still struggle, but I am also giving it my best. I will never give up chasing that person I so badly want to become. It might take me a few years, maybe even the rest of my life, but I'll be dammed if a reach the point where I regret not doing enough with my life. The last thing I want is to settle for something that's less than what I am capable of accomplishing, be it a job, a relationship, or a place. You always have a better choice in life if you are willing to work for it. I am grateful for what I have, but I also know I will always want better for myself. Everyone does.

If you knew how many days you had left to live, would you really live those days by just settling for *good enough*, or would you accept the situation and move forward, making those last days the best days of your life? Wouldn't you want to make your mark on the world? That's why they say *live every day like it's your last.*

I have many hard decisions facing my future self, and sometimes I feel that I don't know where to start. I *do* know one thing: a year is a long time, and there is so much that can be done. I never again want to feel helpless, stuck—one day at a time, I am going to change exactly what I intend to, always working toward my *almost perfect.*

I strive for the feeling between good and perfect: the contentedness of listening to your favorite music on the way to work to face an exciting new day, the gratification of having another chance, the satisfaction of accomplishing your tasks for the day. I strive to capture the expectation of a fun weekend or a tropical vacation, the warmness of staying positive in the face of challenges.

It is the excitement of planning a special occasion, the way you feel counting down the days. It is the thankfulness of being with the people you love and knowing they love you back. It is the blessedness of a safe home, a car to drive, and a warm meal. It is the nostalgia of the past and the eager anticipation of the future.

Don't you see? No matter what we do, there is good in everything, and the bad exists only to make us so much stronger.

When life throws punches, all you have to say is, "I've got this." Because "life loves me, life loves me not" becomes a never-ending cycle of our humanity, no matter the situation.

With one hundred fleeting moments passing you by, be adventurous: in life and in reading.

40324031R00093

Made in the USA
Middletown, DE
25 March 2019